BREAKING A HORSE TO HARNESS

A Step-by-Step Guide

This photograph shows the author driving her pony team to a Roof Seat Break.

Cottenham Loretto, a registered Connemara gelding, who modelled for the majority of the illustrations in this book, is in the position of off-wheeler. His younger brother, Cottenham Lorenzo, is in off-lead. The nearside leader is Alibi, the home-bred daughter of Ali who is also seen in these pages. Her younger sister, Razali, is in near-wheel.

All four ponies were broken by the method described throughout this book.

Miss Anne Muir is on the box seat. Mr Sandy Macnab, the Connemara ponies' breeder, is on the break seat with Mrs Deidre Gordon next to him. Mrs Gordon's daughter, Fiona, is behind, with Mrs June Hales next to her.

Breaking a Horse to Harness
A STEP-BY-STEP GUIDE

Sallie Walrond

J. A. ALLEN : LONDON

This book is dedicated to Mr Sanders Watney,
President of The British Driving Society since
its formation in 1957.

By the same author
A GUIDE TO DRIVING HORSES (Pelham Books)
LOOKING AT CARRIAGES (Pelham Books)
FUNDAMENTALS OF PRIVATE DRIVING (British Driving
Society)
THE ENCYCLOPAEDIA OF CARRIAGE DRIVING
(J. A. Allen)

British Library Cataloguing in Publication Data
Walrond, Sallie
  Breaking a horse to harness.
  1. Draft horses
  2. Harness
  I. Title
  636.1′4   SF311
  ISBN 0 85131 475 9

First published in Great Britain by Pelham Books 1981

This edition published in 1989 by
J. A. Allen & Company Limited
1 Lower Grosvenor Place, Buckingham Palace Road
London SW1W 0EL

Printed in Great Britain by
St Edmundsbury Press Ltd, Bury St Edmunds, Suffolk

CONTENTS

ACKNOWLEDGEMENTS

The author would like to thank Mrs Deirdre Gordon, Miss Anne Grimshaw, Mrs June Hales, and Mr and Mrs Sanders Watney for reading the text and for their valuable suggestions.

She would also like to thank Mrs Gordon, Mrs Hales and Mrs Barbara Taylor for their help on the day when the majority of the photographs were shot.

She is grateful to Charles Goodsman for taking such trouble with the photographs upon which this book is based.

She thanks the following people for permission to use their photographs: Charles Donaldson — back cover photograph, photos 66 and 72; The *East Anglian Daily Times* — frontispiece; 'Eventer' — 67; Mr Peter le Neve Foster — 68, 69 and 70; Miss Daphne Machin Goodall — cover photo, 1, 2, 31, 47 and 56; Mr Frank Morrow — the fly-leaf photograph; and Mr W. S. Pearson — 71; also Mrs N. Bell and Mrs J. D. Greene for allowing their animals and vehicles to be used as models.

She is grateful to Miss Anne Grahame-Johnstone for her line drawings.

She also thanks Mrs Derek Hatley for checking and typing the manuscript and for her advice.

Introductory Considerations

There are no mysteries to breaking a horse to harness. There is absolutely no reason why an averagely competent horseman cannot train his own horse.

Parents are frequently faced with the problem of being saddled with an ageing, much-loved, outgrown family pony. Such an animal is likely to have taught several children to ride and is perhaps now too small for even the youngest. The family cannot bear the prospect of parting with their pet but he cannot be left redundant to get fat in the field and perhaps develop laminitis. Ponies generally do not like being left to do nothing whilst other animals are taken out. They feel that they are missing the fun in which they used to participate.

There is no reason why such a pony should not be trained to pull a cart. He can then, once again, be enjoyed by all the members of the family.

It is quite likely that he has been regularly hunted, pony clubbed and adorned with multiple trappings for fancy dress classes. So, providing that he is introduced carefully to the new idea of harness work he will probably be pleased to co-operate.

The only animals who should not be driven are those which are inveterate kickers and those who are bad in traffic. An animal who kicks, as a natural reaction to anything which frightens him, may revert to his old habit one day when he is in a cart. It is not a pleasant experience to sit helplessly in a vehicle whilst the motive power proceeds to demolish the dashboard and splinter bar before he makes contact with the driver and passenger.

Modern roads with their fast-moving traffic do not accommodate horses who are bad in traffic. Car drivers today are not generally familiar with the way in which a horse's mind works. They do not allow for the fact that a horse is likely to shy out into the road, without warning, as they drive rapidly past a carriage with only a couple of inches between their car and the hub cap. Only animals who are one hundred per cent quiet in traffic are safe to drive on modern roads. Even they can jump into the path of an oncoming car if something unexpectedly frightens them on the side of the road.

Generally speaking, horses or ponies with Arab or Thoroughbred blood in their veins are more difficult to train for harness work than those with mountain and moorland or Hackney breeding.

The animals which are easiest to break are those who have been bred by their trainers or bought as foals with harness work in mind. Their education is started from the day they are born in that they gradually learn some words of command and they are well handled. Training progresses without their really realizing that it is happening.

It is best to work the youngster as a two-year-old for an introductory period to harness. Of course, great care must be taken not to strain the animal in any way. The daily sessions need only last for about twenty minutes and must be executed in good conditions. Muddy or slippery surfaces should be avoided otherwise muscles may get strained or the horse may fall and hurt himself. When he is put to a cart it must be one which is very light. He should only be asked to walk and only be taken for a few hundred yards. Hills must be avoided. If hills cannot be missed, owing to the nature of the terrain, then someone must be available to push the cart up the hill and hold it back down the hill. It will almost certainly be found that the horse can be taken to the stage of pulling a cart at the walk, in a few weeks, if he has a natural aptitude for harness work. He can then be turned away for a year to grow and develop with the comforting knowledge that the youngster has a future ahead as a harness horse.

When he is brought up again, twelve months later, as a three-year-old, he will remember all that which he was taught in the previous year. It must be realized that he will remember the bad things as well as the good things so it is important to make certain that the two-year-old's education is carried out carefully and correctly. Then, when he is worked a year later there should not be any problems. If, however, something dramatic happens during his training as a two-year-old which causes him to become very frightened, the problem will almost surely be there a year later when he is brought up again. It is no good thinking that he can be turned away to forget whatever it was which was causing the trouble because there is an almost certain guarantee that he will not have forgotten anything.

Therefore, it is essential to conclude the two-year-old's stage of education on a day when he has worked obediently and calmly in a relaxed manner. He will then go away with happy thoughts in his head and will probably be disappointed when he finds out that he is not going to be asked to work on the following day.

It is interesting to see three-year-olds who, having been turned away for a year, are obedient and willing to carry out the requests of their trainer within a few minutes of being put on the lungeing rein on the circle.

It is important not to work a three-year-old too hard. The horse is still very young and his joints and back may suffer if they are subjected to too much strain. There is often a temptation to work a three-year-old excessively if he is going quietly, and this must be avoided. It is for this reason that shows which are affiliated to the British Driving Society and combined driving events which are affiliated to the British Horse Society do not allow horses to compete under four years old.

Some people claim that it is inadvisable to start training the youngster until he is four or five years old, arguing that the horse should be left to grow before he is worked. This, of course, can apply to a very backward animal but generally speaking if the youngster is left until he is four or five years old, before he is broken, he will probably cause his trainer considerable trouble. The horse will be shattered by the sudden disturbance of his peace. Fear will cause him to resist and a battle will probably result. A strong, unbroken five-year-old is not much fun to handle and 'training' really does become 'breaking'.

The most important ingredients which are needed for training a horse are time and patience. It takes time to build up mutual confidence and this cannot be achieved in a hurry. Patience is essential. If the trainer ever loses his temper, the horse will become frightened. Nothing will be gained but a tremendous lot may be lost. It could perhaps take months to repair the mental damage

11

which may be done to a horse in a moment of temper from the handler.

If time is limited, on a particular day, it is best to work the horse in a way which is familiar to him so that there is no danger of resistance. He cannot be taken back to his stable if he is refusing to co-operate with his trainer because this will teach him that he has only to resist and he will get his own way. So, if time is limited he should not be asked a question which may cause trouble. Also, if the trainer is under pressure for time he is more likely to become impatient. It is better by far to give the horse a day off than to chance having trouble.

A vehicle and harness will have to be purchased, so therefore it is probably best to get the harness first and take the horse up to the stage of pulling a motor tyre (as described later in the book) before investing a large amount of money in a vehicle. By then the trainer will know whether or not the horse is showing signs of adapting himself to harness work.

It is essential to use sound harness and is probably safest to go to a reputable harness maker to get either a new working set or a good secondhand set. There are now available a number of types of webbing and buffalo hide exercise harness which are quite adequate for training. This type of harness is far safer than an old set which might be picked up relatively cheaply at a sale. There is the chance that it could be rotten in such vital places as the rein billets, hame strap, back-band or traces. Repairs to such items could prove to be very expensive. A breakage caused by neglecting to attend to necessary repairs could result in a bad or even fatal accident.

A two-wheeled vehicle is safer than a four-wheeler for the early stages of single horse driving. A four-wheeler can articulate and may turn over if a horse continues to swing round. Many beginners lean towards purchasing a Governess Cart. Although this type of vehicle is ideal for taking children out for drives it is not really suitable for breaking a horse to harness. Mounting and dismounting by the rear step, and having to open and shut the door, are distinct disadvantages. Also, perhaps more important is the fact that the driver has to sit sideways whilst facing forward. This position, with lack of purchase for the feet, is not ideal for coping with a difficult youngster.

Bits and Bitting

It is stated earlier in this book that there are no mysteries in training a horse for harness. The same applies to bits and bitting. Finding the right bit to suit a particular animal is largely a matter of common sense and determination on the part of the trainer. Careful thought must be given to any problem which may have to be solved. The cause of the trouble might be conformational or mental. Not all mouth problems are caused by bitting. They can be created by the presence of wolf teeth or by the fact that a youngster is changing his teeth. He may have loose milk teeth, and new permanent teeth coming through, which are making his gums sore.

It must be remembered that horses are individuals and that there is a lot of truth in the old saying that 'there is a key to every horse's mouth'.

Care should be taken to select a bit which is suitable for the size and shape of the animal's mouth. It must fit correctly if the horse is going to be comfortable and work happily.

One which is too narrow in the mouthpiece for the horse will pinch. Such a bit with long upper cheeks from the mouthpiece to the top eye will also press against the molars.

A straight bar bit which is too wide will slide from one side of the mouth to the other. A jointed bit which is too large will hang down towards the central incisors and cause discomfort.

Bits are, and have been, made from hundreds of designs for a variety of reasons to give different types of action. Many are named after their designers or place of origin.

Mouthpieces can be made of metals such as steel, stainless steel, nickel, eglantine and aluminium, as well as of rubber, vulcanite and leather. They can also be plated with such metals as chromium and even gold.

Designs of mouthpieces range from jointed, half-moon (or mullen) and straight bar to those with a variety of ports differing in height from about ½ inch (12mm) to 4 inches (100mm) in very extreme cases.

Cheekpieces of curb bits vary in length from about 2 inches

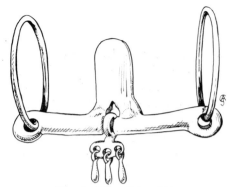

Fig. 1   Mouthing bit

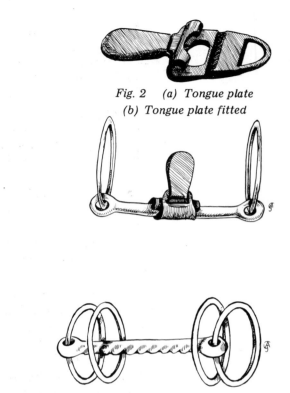

Fig. 2   (a) Tongue plate
         (b) Tongue plate fitted

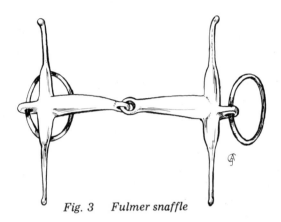

Fig. 3   Fulmer snaffle

Fig. 4   Wilson snaffle (straight bar)

(50mm), to those with long and ornate designs of up to about 9 inches (230mm). Extremely long-cheeked curbs are now rarely used, as are very high ports.

Basically, the actions of bits fall into six groups: jointed, straight bar, half-moon, ported, curb and gag.

A jointed bit acts on the corners and outer sides of the bars of the horse's mouth. It also gives a nutcracker action. Mouthpieces of jointed bits vary enormously in severity. Those with a thick mouthpiece are considerably milder than those with thin mouthpieces. Some jointed bits have mouthpieces which are twisted to give additional severity. Jointed bits can be made milder by a covering of vulcanite or rubber on either side of the joint.

Fig. 5   Wilson snaffle (jointed)

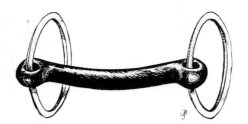

Fig. 6   Half-moon vulcanite snaffle

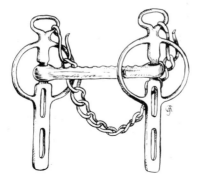

Fig. 7   Liverpool bit (straight bar). The bit shown here has the rough side towards the tongue, which is more severe than the usual arrangement where the smooth side is towards the tongue.

Fig. 8   Liverpool bit with low port

16

A straight bar bit lies flat on the tongue, which takes a great percentage of the pressure with the remainder being taken on the bars of the mouth. Some bits with a straight bar have a rough side and a smooth side so that they can be reversed according to the degree of severity required.

A half-moon bit lies over the curve of the tongue and more of the pressure is taken on the bars than with a straight bit.

Horses with fleshy or tender tongues often prefer to have a bit with a low port. This relieves a considerable amount of the pressure from the tongue and transfers more to the bars of the mouth. Many horses will flex their jaws and go kindly in a bit with a low port, whilst they will resist in one which has a straight bar.

Bits with curb cheeks and curb chains are designed in a variety of ways to work on a leverage system. The lower down the bar that the reins are buckled, the more severe the bit becomes. If the rein is buckled onto the ring (i.e. 'plain cheek'), the action is identical to that of a snaffle. When the reins are buckled onto one of the bars down the cheek there will be leverage on the mouth once the reins are pulled.

The curb chain should be fastened so that it lies flat in the chin groove. When the cheek of the bit lies level with the horse's mouth, the curb chain should hang loosely against the chin groove. When the cheek of the bit is tilted back to an angle of 45° with the horse's mouth, the curb chain should tighten against the chin groove to encourage the horse to give with his jaw and flex. As the lower part of the bit tilts back, so the upper part goes forward. This puts pressure onto the cheekpieces of the bridle through the upper eyes of the bit, which encourages the horse to bend at the poll and lower his head. Some curb bits have a swivel at the mouthpiece to prevent such pressure being transmitted to the poll. Many curb bits are made with mouthpieces which have ports of varying heights. Some are designed merely to take the pressure off the horse's tongue. Others are designed with a high port to make the bit more severe. Such bits have a port of up to about 4 inches (100mm) in height, which acts against the roof of the mouth. Therefore, if the reins are buckled onto the bottom slots of a long-cheeked curb bit with a high port, the arrangement is very

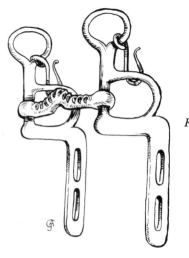

Fig. 9   Elbow bit

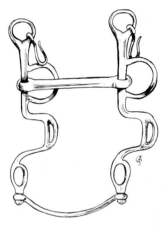

Fig. 10   Buxton bit

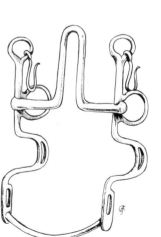

Fig. 11   High-port Buxton bit

18

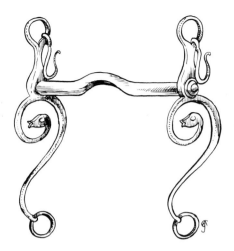

Fig. 12 Snake-cheeked curb bit

Fig. 13 Pulley bridoon

severe. It can be made even stronger by tightening the noseband in order to keep the horse's mouth shut.

High ports are seldom employed nowadays and are usually inadvisable. Their only use for breaking would be to prevent the horse from getting his tongue over the bit and in that application would never be used in conjunction with a curb. If such a bit is used with the reins buckled onto plain cheek (or ring) then the bit is mild. There will be no leverage, curb action, poll pressure or action onto the roof of the mouth. So, although a bit such as a Buxton may appear, to the novice, to be very severe, it can be extremely mild if the curb is not used.

It is commonly thought, by newcomers, that it is preferable to keep a young horse in a jointed snaffle for a considerable time in preference to a Liverpool bit. In fact, once the youngster has learnt the rudiments of stopping and turning, which are best taught in a Fulmer snaffle, he may well find the straight bar of a Liverpool to be more comfortable. The curb chain can be fitted loosely so that it is non-operative. It need not even be made of chain. Some horses, with sensitive chin grooves, are happier in a curb 'chain' which has either a leather or an elastic centre and links on either side for adjustment. Sheepskin or rubber tubing can be threaded over the chain to lessen the severity.

A curb bit with an elbow-shaped cheek is useful with a horse who catches hold of the cheeks of an ordinary curb with his lips.

The only type of gag which is normally used for harness work is a pulley bridoon which is incorporated with a bearing rein.

The mildest type of bit is probably a rubber half-moon snaffle. The most severe would be a long-cheeked, high-ported curb when the reins are buckled onto bottom bar and the noseband is fastened tightly.

Some horses prefer to have the mouthpiece of a straight bar bit softened a little. This can be achieved by winding a thin bandage around the bit or by covering it with either a piece of inner tubing or chamois leather. A coating of honey or golden syrup over such a covering will encourage a dry-mouthed horse to salivate.

Once the 'key' to the horse's mouth has been found, it is best to keep that kind of bit for all his work.

PHOTO 1 **A Bridle With a Liverpool Bit**

Here can be seen a correctly fitting bridle with a Liverpool bit. The reins are buckled to their most severe position, which is known as bottom bar, giving the greatest leverage onto the mouth. The flatness of the curb chain should be noted.

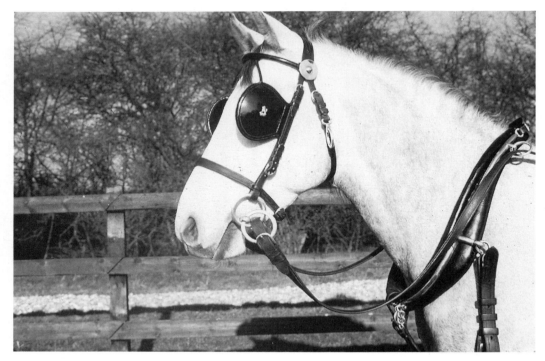

PHOTO 2 **A Bridle With a Wilson Snaffle Bit**

This photograph shows Ali wearing a Wilson snaffle. The reins are buckled onto both rings which is the mildest way of attaching them. The headpiece is buckled onto the floating rings on the bit. If the reins are buckled only to the rings which are attached to the mouthpiece, the action of the bit is much more severe. When tension is put onto the reins, the jointed bit forms a nutcracker shape and the floating rings are pressed against the sides of the mouth causing pinching against the molars. A few people drive with one rein buckled onto both rings and the other buckled onto just the bit ring. This can be very severe, if used roughly. It is known as 'cab fashion'.

The Use of Aromatics

It is common knowledge that fear travels down the reins like electricity and that if a handler is nervous the feeling of apprehension is instantly transmitted to the horse. Various theories are put forward relating to how this state of affairs is passed from the human to the animal. Obviously, if a nervous person is holding the reins the simple explanation is that the tension will be felt by the horse, through his mouth, causing him to react accordingly. If the horse is young, or uncertain, he will probably become jumpy and hesitant. If he is a cold-blooded, solid type he will quite likely just take charge of the person who is trying to control him. It has been proved, frequently, that a nervous passenger sitting in a carriage, or an agitated person merely standing alongside a sensitive horse, can cause havoc although neither one of them is touching or speaking to the animal concerned. A calm assistant will, without doubt, be an asset to the trainer by his mere presence in a situation which might otherwise be fraught. A confident trainer usually produces a willing generous horse who, through complete trust, is prepared to go anywhere and do whatever is asked of him without question.

Fear is transmitted from the human to the horse by smell. If the trainer is apprehensive, a flow of adrenalin is released from the adrenal glands in order to put the body into top gear to deal with the forthcoming challenge. A person does not have to be actually frightened for there to be adrenalin in the blood stream; anticipation of having to do something difficult can be quite enough.

The smell of adrenalin is instantly recognized by the horse as a warning of danger. Naturally, this results in immediate lack of confidence which quickly becomes mutual.

It is a well-known fact that bee-keepers can work amongst their hives in comparative safety whereas a nervous visitor will almost certainly get stung. Equally, anyone who is afraid of dogs is usually greeted with raised hackles and a disagreeable mouth, whilst a confident person will be met with a smiling expression and a wagging tail.

There are numerous stories, handed down for generations,

about the uses of calming oils and secret potions which were employed by men who spent their lives with working horses. Many of the stallion walkers apparently used aromatics of varying kinds.

All kinds of mysterious theories were suggested which made the handlers appear to have some kind of magical power over their horses. Tales of frogs' bones, witches (or hag) stones and horse whisperers have been related.

The real answer to the mystery appears to be quite simple. The smell of adrenalin, which is emitted by the handler whenever any trouble is expected, should be masked by an equine aromatic.

Unfortunately, most of the old recipes seem to have been lost; others contain ingredients which are now unobtainable.

Fortunately, there is now available a product known as 'Pax' which is effective. It can be obtained from Day, Son and Hewitt of Grant Street, Bradford, Yorkshire. A little is rubbed onto the hands and forehead before the horse is approached. He will immediately become attracted to his handler. He is not able to smell any adrenalin which may be present. In turn, because the horse is calm, the handler is confident and the whole situation changes.

Psychologists probably have all kinds of answers to this theory, but it has been proved by the author, for well over fifteen years and with a large number of animals, that the use of Pax makes horses much easier to handle on certain occasions.

A lot of people hotly deny that they are ever nervous, claiming that they never experience the slightest feeling of tension. Surely, if the trainer has any feeling at all, he is fairly certain to experience at least a small amount of apprehension, when the horse is put to a cart for the first time? It is the most dangerous operation in any form of horse breaking; far more so than when a horse is ridden for the first time. No chances can be taken. If the horse becomes frightened and gets away, he will not stop until he has kicked himself out of the cart. The vehicle will be smashed, the harness will be broken and the horse will probably be ruined for life as far as work in harness is concerned. Once a horse has kicked himself out of a cart he may well never be of any more use for pleasure driving.

These thoughts must inevitably cause adrenalin to flow through the body of the handler. The use of Pax has the effect of calming both the trainer and the horse. The handler will be aware that the possible smell of adrenalin is masked and will relax. The horse, in turn, will react accordingly and remain calm. The trainer, then realizing that the horse is not upset, will become more confident and the whole situation will be less fraught.

It is advisable to persuade all helpers or onlookers to put a little Pax onto their hands, so that the smell of adrenalin cannot be picked up from an assistant.

It must be remembered, though, that Pax will not work like magic. It will not, for instance, turn a traffic-shy horse into one which will face heavy lorries, nor will it result in making a horse jump red walls when he has previously refused to do so. It will, however, prevent the horse from smelling that the driver or rider is afraid of the lorry, or the wall, before it is approached. Therefore if the correct training procedure is executed at home there is a chance that, with the help of the aromatic, the animal may eventually be persuaded to face up to that which was frightening him.

PHOTO 3 **The Arena**

The whole procedure of breaking will be much easier if an enclosed arena is constructed. If an indoor school or manège is not available then a suitable training place must be made. It is essential to choose a flat area of about 60 feet (20m) in diameter. If the arena is not level it will be impossible to obtain correct and even paces. The horse will tend to rush down the hill on one side of the circle and labour up the other side. The simplest school can be made by using fences or hedges which already exist, as seen in this illustration. Here, one side of the arena is formed by a substantial hedge and a second side by post and rail fencing. On no account should a barbed wire fence be used as a barrier. The horse will almost certainly get caught in it at some time during training. Or, if he does not actually get into it he is sure to damage

26

his harness by going too close when his blinkers will prevent him from seeing how near he is.

Interlocking hurdles, which are seen here, are ideal for making the other two sides of the enclosure. They can be put up quite easily and do not have to be permanent. Jump stands and poles are also useful for constructing a ring.

When the arena is first used, particular attention must be paid to keeping the horse on a true circle. The exact centre should be marked with ashes, or similar, and the trainer must stand on it so that a circular track is worn round the edge. Horses must be prevented from coming into the centre of the arena, apart from when they are being brought into the middle for a change of rein. The result of this careful early administration will be a grass arena with a circular perimeter track which young horses will automatically follow, making the early days of training much easier for all concerned.

It is interesting to note that every two-year-old unbroken horse which is taken into the school illustrated, goes happily round on the lunge within a few minutes. For this reason, early training causes no distress or strain and great confidence is built between horse and handler.

It is not advisable to try to work an unbroken horse in an open field. Difficulties will almost certainly be encountered and the lessons will become a battle. There is absolutely no need for battles in breaking. The horse's greater strength must be overcome by the trainer's superior intelligence and guile.

Horses which are worked at the beginning in a large open space will probably tend to lean on the lunge rein. This will lead to stiffness throughout the whole body and result in untrue paces. In a desperate attempt to hang on to the unbroken horse, the trainer will haul the animal's head towards the centre of the circle. The horse, in response, will probably either turn to face his trainer and refuse to go round, or pull harder away from his handler. He will then be likely to trot round on three sets of tracks instead of two. If, for instance, he is going on a left-handed circle and trying to hang out, he will be seen to go with his near-fore on one set of tracks, his off-fore and near-hind on another, and his off-hind on a third set. His whole spine will become stiff and he will be learning how strong he is and how easy it is to evade his trainer.

Another resistance which the horse may use if he is worked in the open, is to hang out on the side of the circle which is nearest to the stable or field gate. He will probably then fall in on the opposite side. This will result in an oval-shaped figure instead of a circle.

If training is carried out in an enclosed arena these evasions will not occur. The perimeter fencing can be used to hold the horse onto the circle whilst the rein is kept slack. The horse never learns to lean away from the trainer and never becomes heavy in the hand. This all helps to make a light-mouthed, supple horse. Horses who learn to set their necks at an early age often later set their jaws and have hard mouths.

Any tendency to fall into the centre of the arena can be prevented by the trainer positioning himself in such a way that judicious use of the whip will hold the horse onto the track. The horse will soon learn that he is not allowed to cut across the arena and will give up trying.

PHOTO 4 **The Cavesson**

The horse should wear just a cavesson for the first stages of his training. The heavy-duty, old-fashioned kind is best. This has a thickly padded metal-reinforced nosepiece. Before the cavesson is put on, all three straps which fasten round the underneath of the jaw should be unbuckled. It is a help to leave the headcollar round the horse's neck, so that the trainer has some means of holding on to the horse if he tries to walk away. The cavesson is placed over the front of the horse's face and the headpiece is passed over the ears. If the horse objects to this, the cheekpiece can be undone to enable the headpiece to be passed behind the ears before being buckled down to the cheekpiece. The nose-band should be buckled tightly enough to secure it firmly round the horse's nose. One which is buckled too loosely will get pulled off the centre of the nose and will be ineffective. The lower throatlash should be fastened tighter than a normal throatlash otherwise the outer cheek piece of the cavesson will get pulled into the outer eye. The top throatlash should be buckled short enough to prevent the cavesson from coming off if the horse should pull away from his trainer.

The lunge rein should be buckled to the centre ring at the front of the noseband. This gives the greatest control because the horse's head can then be turned towards the trainer much more easily than if the rein is fixed to one of the side rings which are fitted to some cavessons. The lunge rein should have a swivel at the buckling end to prevent it from getting twisted. The rein is best if it is made from tubular webbing and it should be at least 26 feet (8m) long. Nylon lunge reins must be avoided, as should those of single webbing. Both can give horrible rope burns to the trainer's hand if the horse snatches away suddenly. Brass clips should not be used as they are inclined to break if they are put under sudden strain. A leather billet with a steel buckle is the safest.

A bridle and bit should never be employed for the first stages of training. The handler will find that he has far greater control over an unbroken animal with a correctly fitting breaking cavesson than if the horse, with an unmade mouth, wears a bridle. An unmade mouth can feel far less responsive than a hard mouth. The horse will resist the pain inflicted by the bit because he will not yet have learnt how to relax and give his jaw in response to his handler. He will probably become frightened and even violent. He may resort to rearing and throw himself over backwards. Once he has learnt how effective that can be in getting his own way, he will become very difficult to train. Alternatively he may just lower his head and take charge as a method of escaping the pressure on his sensitive tongue and bars.

Lungeing

Serious training starts with lungeing.

A horse which has been well handled from the time that he was born will be far easier to lunge than one which has been left untouched. An unhandled youngster will be afraid of the trainer and a lot of time will have to be spent in building up the initial confidence before any real progress can be made. Even the act of putting the breaking cavesson onto a young horse who has not been accustomed to having a headcollar or halter slipped over his ears can cause a problem. So life will be much easier for all concerned if the youngster has been firmly and sensibly handled from the day that he was born. He should be used to having a head-collar put on and must have been led from both sides. It is a good idea to lead the foal from the offside whenever the thought occurs. This will probably result in him being led equally from both sides. There is the tendency always to approach a horse from the nearside, which is a great mistake. If a horse grows to two or three years old before anyone goes up to him or leads him from the offside, he will be very difficult to persuade to go on the right rein and may always be one-sided.

The purposes of work on the lunge are numerous. The pupil must be taught to obey the commands of his trainer. This entails teaching the animal a limited amount of words. He must be made to understand the meaning of 'Walk', 'Trot', 'Canter', 'Steady', 'Go on' and 'Whoa'. The command 'Whoa' is probably preferable to 'Halt' or 'Stand' since it is the one most likely to be used by a layman to stop a horse, and so should be useful in the horse's vocabulary. It is by patient repetition at the right time that these words will eventually be understood. They should each be said with a slightly different tone to help the horse to learn what is required. The 'increase of pace' words are best said with a sharper intonation to the voice, and the 'slowing down' words with a more drawn out sound. It is a help if these words have been used during the early days of leading the animal in hand from when he was a foal. Horses are not always blessed with great intelligence but they do have remarkably good memories.

It is best not to include the sound of a 'click' of the tongue in the horse's vocabulary. He should not be trained to respond to a click to go forward for it will be found that some spectators sometimes click to horses to urge them on when seeing them driven. If the animal has never been trained to react to the noise he will ignore it. If, however, his trainer has used this signal for telling him to go forward the horse may mistake it for a command from his driver (as one click can sound like another), and jump forward unexpectedly. His driver may not have heard the offending 'click' and an accident may follow. It is far better to urge the horse on with a forward sounding command like 'Go on'. Horses who have been trained to go forward in response to a 'click' can also easily become upset in the show ring by another driver clicking to his horse to encourage him to extend as he overtakes a rival competitor and the first horse, which was already going forward correctly, on hearing an unexpected 'click' may break pace. His driver may be taken unaware by the increased impulsion and he may not react quickly enough to prevent the break. Such an incident could lose an exhibitor an important award if the judge happens to be looking at that moment — meanwhile the cause of the trouble perhaps goes on to win the class!

It is important to be able to differentiate between the horse misunderstanding what is required and blatantly disobeying the wishes of his trainer. If he is punished for not doing what he is told, when he simply misunderstood what was required, he will soon become muddled and afraid. A horse should never be chastized unnecessarily. It is essential that the trainer always controls his temper. Once a horse becomes really frightened he loses his sense of reason. It can take a very long time to regain the confidence which may have been lost in a matter of a few seconds. In extreme cases, the horse may never be the same again. There are instances of horses which have been known to be quiet and amenable until experiencing some unreasonable exploitation which has transformed them into vicious animals. Very few horses are born bad, though of course some have much calmer temperaments than others.

Careful work at the walk, trot and canter, in both directions, on the lunge will develop correct paces. The horse will learn to go freely and calmly forward. He will discover how to balance himself on the circle. His muscles will begin to develop into the desired form. A ewe-necked horse can sometimes be transformed into one with a pleasing top line if the correct work is executed. One such two-year-old, which was broken by the author, altered so much that a few years later he ended up in the ribbons at Wembley in a show hunter class.

Perhaps the most important reason of all for work on the lunge is that confidence and mutual trust, which is the foundation of all future work, will gradually develop between the pupil and the trainer.

The First Lesson

It is a help if the horse is given some idea of what is going to be required before he is taken out into the arena for his first lesson. He can be introduced to the idea of lungeing in his loose box, which should be deeply bedded for this purpose.

The cavesson and lunge rein are put on. The lunge rein should be taken in the left hand with the loop end held first and the rein carefully looped up in lengths of about 2 feet (60cm), so that the part of the rein which is nearest to the horse's head is lying uppermost in the hand. This enables it to run out freely if the horse should jump away. A tangled mass of webbing wound round the hand can be very dangerous. Fingers can easily be broken or even pulled off by a sudden and violent movement.

The lunge whip is held in the right hand. The light, nylon kind is best. A heavy, steel-lined whip can become very tiring and make the wrist ache. On no account should the trainer be tempted to use his holly driving whip for lungeing. It will, without doubt, get broken in a very short time. Holly whips are, in any case, not suitable for lungeing.

The horse forms the third part of a triangle as he is told to 'Walk on'. The first two sides are formed by the lunge rein and whip. The horse is sent round the box and will almost certainly go quite happily. Then, when he is required to stop, the trainer should step in front of him and say 'Whoa', being sure to keep the whip pointing downwards. The horse must then be rewarded and caressed so that he understands that his trainer is pleased with what he has just done. The horse is then led into the middle of the loose box. The handler must transfer the lunge rein into his right hand and the whip to his left hand. He will then have to be careful to position himself down the right-hand side of the horse before attempting to ask him to move off in a clockwise, i.e. right-handed, direction. If the horse has not been handled adequately from the offside, some difficulty will probably be experienced. It is for this reason that this preliminary work in the confined area of a loose box is so necessary. Once the horse has gone round to the right a few times he can be stopped and rewarded. It

PHOTO 5

will be found that it is best *not* to have an assistant to lead the horse as this usually confuses the animal and causes him to take much longer to understand what is required. He does not know to whom he should listen and he may become frightened.

PHOTO 5 **Trotting on the Lunge**

(*The hurdles have been taken down for the purpose of these photographs. The perimeter of the track can be seen by the ridge of grass.*)

Once the horse has gone happily round the loose box in either direction he can be led to the arena in the cavesson.

The horse is taken into the middle of the school. The lunge rein is held in the left hand and the whip is taken in the right hand in order to send the horse off to the left. If the horse should swing away and go off on a right-handed circle on this first occasion, it is best to let him continue and keep him going forward. The rein must quickly be changed to the other hand and the position of the whip altered to keep him going on. It may turn out to be an advantage as it is usually easier to get horses to go off to the left, so less difficulty will be experienced when the time comes to stop and go the other way.

It is very important, in this first attempt at getting the horse to go off on the circle, to position the body in the correct place in relation to the horse. The trainer should stand alongside the horse's shoulder and then when he gives the command 'Walk on' he must step towards the animal's quarters, letting the lunge rein out as the horse goes, and send him forward with the whip. The horse will almost certainly go forward from the trainer and he must not be restricted. If he encounters any resistance from the lunge rein he will probably stop and turn to face his trainer in confusion. It does not matter whether he walks, trots or canters when he goes off on the circle on this occasion, as long as he goes forward. It is a great mistake to check the horse if he canters because he will then be likely to stop, swing round and get muddled. Also, it is best if he does not discover how easy it is to stop and pirouette round, because he will quickly learn that it is a useful and effective evasion.

As mentioned earlier, if the arena has a track around the perimeter, it will be found that the young horse will automatically follow this circular path and there will be no problem in getting him to go round in the beginning. It is usually necessary, though, to walk round, in order to be near the pupil to create enough impulsion to keep him going forward at this early stage. Later, the trainer should aim at standing still in the centre.

The most common fault amongst newcomers to lungeing is that they do not start by positioning themselves in the correct place, so the horse does not go forward. Then, when the bewildered horse does eventually go, they keep him on too tight and short a rein. The novice often tries to hold the horse away from the perimeter barrier. There is no need to keep the horse from the fence. He will not bump into it once he has discovered that it is solid and does not give way. It is far better to let the lunge rein hang in a slight loop. The weight of the rein will give adequate contact to the horse's nose from the trainer's hand. An animal who has been schooled in this way will later go on a lunge rein with a light contact, even when he is being worked in the open. If, however, he learns to use his strength as a resistance against his trainer in these formative lessons, it will probably be almost impossible to lunge him outside a school later on. This will be a nuisance because there are bound to be occasions when it is necessary to lunge him in an open space.

When the horse is going round on the circle it is important that the trainer positions himself slightly behind the horse's shoulder. A novice handler is inclined to get ahead of the horse, which may cause him to stop and difficulties will be encountered. In fact, it is by stepping in front of the horse that he will be taught to halt in his early lessons.

Newcomers to lungeing find that they get dizzy. It is a help to watch the horse's eye instead of his legs. The feeling of dizziness will not persist once the trainer becomes more experienced in lungeing.

The horse should be kept going round to the left at the trot until he understands that he is required to go in a circle round his trainer. This usually takes about five minutes. He should not be kept going for too long in one direction before being sent off in the other because this can create difficulties in persuading him to go the opposite way. The command to walk should be given in a long slow-toned 'W — a — a — l — k'. It is quite likely that the horse will slow down to a walk. He may even stop. He must not be pulled into the centre of the arena but should be kept on the track. If he does stop, although he has been told to walk, it is best to go up to him and make a fuss of him. If he is sent on, on this occasion, he will become confused. He may, of course, just walk round, which is splendid. It often helps to try to transmit some kind of thought waves to the horse. Very often, if the trainer concentrates hard on what he wants from the horse, he will stand more chance of being obeyed. Also, it is sometimes found that if, after a command has been given and the horse is clearly wondering whether to obey or not, the trainer says an encouraging and calm word like 'Good', the horse will realize that his thoughts were correct and he will obey the command.

If the horse is now walking round, he will have to be stopped so that he can be brought into the centre of the arena and made to go off to the right. The halt at this early stage can be achieved by using the tallest barrier at the edge of the arena. In the arena seen here, there is a tree beyond the hedge, which makes the hedge look more impenetrable. As the horse is walking round the arena, at a point coming towards the tree, the command 'Whoa' is given. At the same time, the whip must be lowered. The horse will probably not understand and will continue to walk forward. As the horse comes nearer to the tree, the command 'Whoa' is given again, and the trainer must drop the whip onto the ground and step across to the front of the horse. This will usually result in a rather abrupt halt. The horse will be confused but will soon relax once he is caressed and given a tit-bit. He can then be led into the centre of the arena in preparation for going off in a right-handed direction.

It is a great mistake to pull the horse into the centre of the school in order to stop him because this will teach him that he can come into the middle and dart off in the opposite direction whenever he wants to evade his trainer. This will lead to difficulties later. Also, it will mean that he is not learning to halt on the circle. This work is essential for the harness horse as it is the foundation for standing unheld, which he must do whilst being put to a cart when his training progresses to that stage.

The horse must now be sent off to the right. Great care should be taken to ensure that he goes off at the first attempt. The trainer must be certain to place himself along the right-hand side of the horse and be sure to drive the horse forward with the whip, and not resist him with the rein, as the command to 'Walk on' is given. Once he has gone off, great attention must be paid to keeping him going forward because he will not like going in the direction opposite to the way he was going before. The trainer must be in a position which drives the horse onward. Failure to do

38

this will almost certainly result in the horse stopping and swinging round to go in the anti-clockwise direction.

Once the horse has gone round calmly on the circle for about five minutes he should be told to walk and halt using the same procedure as described earlier. He can then be praised and brought into the centre of the arena before being sent off again on the left rein.

Once he has begun to understand what is required and has worked two or three times in each direction, he can be led back to his stable. The time taken for this first lesson outside can vary from about thirty minutes with a confident well-handled youngster, to an hour, or longer, with an animal who has not been adequately handled from the offside.

It is essential to stop the lesson on a good note so that the horse can be taken back to his box in a contented frame of mind and left to think. It is a great mistake to work the horse for so long that he becomes tired.

The young, unfit and unmuscled horse will soon get weary. Quite naturally, if he begins to ache he will start to resist his trainer. The trainer, in turn, will think that he must keep the horse going until he does as he is told. This can lead to a difficult situation which could have been avoided if the lesson had been stopped earlier.

Once this state of affairs has been created by such circumstances, a battle may begin. Although the trainer may, in the end, win the fight, the horse will probably have discovered how easy it is to use his strength against his trainer. It is important to try to keep the animal willing and happy to co-operate with the requirements of his trainer. The demands on his strength should be kept for when he is asked to give his best during the course of his work in the future and not for resisting his trainer during simple requirements in early breaking.

PHOTO 6 **Cantering on the Lunge**

Although it is not necessary for a harness horse to do much work at the canter, it is advisable to teach him to obey the command. It is not normal for horses which are used for private driving to canter. However, those people who want to scurry drive or compete in combined driving events will wish to canter their pairs and teams for competitions against the clock. So, the horse must be trained on the lunge to canter to command.

The horse should go forward into the canter with the use of the voice backed up by the whip if necessary. If he goes off on the wrong leg, or disunited, it is best to send him forward and he will probably change onto the inner legs automatically. If he is checked when he goes into canter on the wrong leg he will probably become confused, thinking that he was not meant to

40

canter. He will then fail to understand what is required. At a later stage he could be checked if he went on the wrong leg because, by then, he would understand what was meant by the word 'Canter'.

Although it is rather out of context in a book on training a harness horse, it may be of interest to mention a useful method of making a horse lead on the inner leg. This can be used if a horse persistently leads on the outer leg. A small jump is put across the track. This is approached at the trot and, as the horse takes off, the command to canter is given. The horse will then almost certainly land on the inner fore-leg and canter away on the correct leading leg.

The words 'leading leg' are rather misleading because, in fact, the order in which the legs touch the ground (other than when landing over a fence) if the horse is cantering on a right circle are: (1) near-hind; (2) off-hind and near-fore together; (3) off-fore. In watching carefully it will be noticed that the off-fore and off-hind appear to sweep forward, ahead of the nearside legs, which is why they are called the leading legs. A novice horse which canters with the nearside legs leading on a right-handed circle, looks very ungainly and unbalanced and is quite likely to cross his legs, knock himself and fall. In some ridden dressage tests this outer lead is practised and known as counter canter. By that stage of training, the horse is balanced and going correctly so it is not dangerous and does not look so ungainly.

A horse is said to be disunited when his feet touch the ground in the following order: (1) near-hind; (2) off-hind and off-fore; (3) near-fore; *or* (1) off-hind; (2) near-hind and near-fore; (3) off-fore. The pace looks ugly as the horse appears to be leading with one leg in front and the opposite one behind.

PHOTO 7 **Walking on the Lunge**

The walk is a very important pace. The horse should cover the ground with a free regular four-time walk. It must not be hurried as this can lead to an irregular two-time pace when the legs are inclined to move laterally. Neither should it be slow and lack impulsion. Ideally, the track (hoof mark) made by the hind foot should overtake the last track of the front foot as the horse walks freely around the arena in a calm manner with his head reasonably low. A good walk can and should be developed on the lunge. There is often a temptation to neglect this part of a young horse's education as the trainer feels that it is rather boring.

PHOTO 8 **Halt on the Lunge**

This is the essential basic training which will finally result in the horse standing unheld whilst he is being put to, and taken from, his vehicle in later years. It is very important and time must be spent training the horse to halt on the circle when he is requested. The result will be a horse who will stand unheld whenever he is required to do so and, in the years that lie ahead, will be easy to handle at shows or when being driven at home for pleasure.

The technique of initially teaching the horse to halt on the lunge is explained earlier on page 38.

The Introduction to a Stable Roller

It is a good idea to introduce the horse to the feeling of a girth as soon as possible. A stable roller is ideal because this can be left on in the loose box. The padding prevents the horse from getting sore and if he rolls there is nothing to get broken. The roller must be put on carefully and should not be buckled too tightly at first. Some horses become frightened by the restriction which they first feel with the girth. If this is pulled up tightly the horse may stiffen his front legs and hump his back. Then, when he is made to move forward he may plunge round the box. It can even result in the horse throwing himself down. Once he has done this, he is quite likely to use this resistance throughout his life. It is very unpleasant trying to drive a horse which throws himself onto the ground whenever he does not wish to obey his trainer. In fact, a horse who does this, even occasionally, is unfit for harness. So great care must be taken when the roller is first put on. Of course, it must not be so loose that there is danger of it slipping back. If there is any worry that this might happen, it is advisable to put some kind of breast strap round the horse's chest to hold the roller forward.

The horse can be left for an hour or so in the stable wearing the roller. If he objects to its presence, it is a good idea to leave it on for longer. Care must be taken, if he sweats, that he does not get sore under his elbows and become galled.

The Mouthing Bit (see Fig. 1)

A bridle can also be put on at an early stage. A mouthing bit with a tongue plate is useful to prevent the horse from learning to get his tongue over the bit. This can easily become an annoying habit which will be hard to break. In order to escape the pressure of the bit, the horse may draw his tongue down towards his throat. If a jointed bit is used, it is quite easy for the horse to bring his tongue back over the top of the bit. The horse will then be even more uncomfortable and will fuss dramatically. One way of preventing the young horse from getting his tongue over a jointed bit is to tighten the cheekpieces of the bridle so that the bit is placed higher in the mouth. However, this will result in the corners of the horse's mouth being severely wrinkled. They are almost certain to become sore and the horse will then have good reason to fuss. Therefore, in order to avoid this unnecessary discomfort, it is best to use a straight bar bit with a tongue plate which can be placed comfortably in the horse's mouth without wrinkling the corners. He will probably soon learn to accept the feeling of a bit on his tongue and will never discover how to get his tongue over the mouthpiece.

Mouthing bits have three or four small drops of metal dangling from the centre of the mouthpiece which are known as 'keys'. These encourage the horse to move his tongue and salivate. There are divided schools of thought about the value of a mouthing bit. Some experts claim that it makes the horse become too busy with his mouth and teaches him to fidget. The author likes to see a horse with a reasonably wet mouth which is not rigid, and finds that the use of a straight bar, tongue-plated mouthing bit for about five days, in sessions of up to half an hour each, helps to produce light-mouthed, responsive horses who do not fuss with their heads. A horse must never be long-reined, ridden or driven in a mouthing bit and will probably only wear one for a few hours in his whole training.

Horses, like people, are all different and that which suits one at this stage of training may not suit another.

Lungeing in a Roller

Once the horse is working quietly at all paces on the circle in a cavesson and is reasonably obedient, he can be taken into the arena wearing a stable roller. As he has been getting used to this indoors it will probably not cause too much worry. If he does hump his back and plunge he must be sent forward. He should not be punished or stopped. He is probably afraid and is trying to rid himself of the restriction which he is feeling. The trainer should try to pretend that he has not noticed the behaviour and should just keep the horse going on.

If the horse canters round kicking, it is best not to tell him to trot or walk because it is unlikely that he will obey. He will not be listening to his trainer and any words of command are going to be ignored. It is therefore better to stand still quietly and let him tear round. When he is obviously going to reduce pace it is a good plan to say 'T r o — o — t — t'. He will quite likely obey and then the trainer can say 'Good'. If the horse clearly has no intention of walking, he must be kept trotting and even sent forward into canter again before being asked eventually to trot and then walk. By this time he will quite likely be pleased to slow down and listen. It is useless and very harmful to give instructions which are clearly going to be disobeyed, as this only teaches the horse that he has superior strength and does not have to obey if he does not want to. The aim in training is eventually to make the horse think that he must obey, without question, the demands of his trainer. The horse must be worked at all paces, in both directions, and kept going until he settles.

The bridle, with the mouthing bit, can also be put on at this stage. It will be found that it is possible to put the bridle, without a noseband, on top of the cavesson. Care must be taken to keep the noseband of the cavesson high above the bit, so that pinching does not occur at the corners of the mouth. The lunge rein is attached to the cavesson as before.

PHOTOS 9–10 **Trotting and Walking in the Driving Saddle**

PHOTO 9
*Trotting in the
driving saddle.*

Once the horse has accepted working in a stable roller on the circle and the trainer is able to girth this up to a reasonable tightness, without the horse resisting, the driving saddle can be put onto the pupil for work in the arena. On no account should the saddle be left on the horse whilst he is loose in the stable. If he rolls he will almost certainly bend the terrets and he could break the tree of the saddle.

Providing that he has settled thoroughly to the feel of the roller, there is no reason why he should object to the saddle.

When the horse is going calmly, as seen in Photo 10, he is ready to go on to the next stage.

47

PHOTO 10

*Walking in the
driving saddle.*

The Crupper

It is a good idea to leave the horse standing in the stable wearing a crupper before he is taken outside and worked in it in the arena. Some horses object strongly to wearing a crupper. Care must be taken to introduce the pupil gently to this piece of equipment. It is essential to use a crupper which is soft. One which is hard will probably chafe the sensitive skin under the horse's tail. The inside of a crupper dock is usually filled with linseed to keep it pliable. Even so, it is quite a good plan to cover the tail piece with an off-cut of sheepskin to make it more comfortable for the young horse.

The stable roller and possibly a breast girth should be put on. The crupper can be attached to the centre of the roller and tied in place with baler twine.

Great care must be taken when the crupper is put on to see that the hairs at the top of the dock are not caught under the crupper, as this can cause great discomfort. It is important to make sure that the crupper is high up against the top of the dock. One which is put on too low may become dislodged and in any case will be uncomfortable.

The horse can be left in the stable for an hour or so to get used to the feeling of pressure under his tail. Horses which are very frightened should be left for a longer time in the stable before being taken out into the arena to work in a crupper. Extreme cases may have to be left overnight, but this is very unusual. If a horse has to be left for long periods before he will accept the crupper, care must be taken to ensure that he does not become sore under his tail.

PHOTO 11   **The Saddle and Crupper at the Trot**

When the horse has accepted wearing the crupper in the stable, it can be buckled to the driving saddle and the horse can be brought out into the arena to be lunged. As when he was first brought out wearing the roller, if the horse objects to the crupper and reacts by kicking and bucking, he should not be punished. It does no good to chastize him as it will only make him more frightened. He is probably only kicking because he is trying to remove the unwanted appendage. He must be sent on and kept going forward until he settles. Once he finds that he cannot kick the crupper off, he will accept the fact that he has got to put up with its presence.

50

PHOTO 12　**The Saddle and Crupper at the Canter**

It is important to work the horse at the canter at this stage. Very often a youngster will go quietly with the crupper at the walk and trot but will explode at the canter. If this is likely to happen, it is safest to get it over now and not wait until the horse is put to a cart and one day canters because something has frightened him. Once he starts to kick, if he is put to, he is almost certain to contact the splinter bar. The ensuing fright is likely to result in disaster. So, this must be avoided. Therefore, it is best to let the youngster find out, whilst he is on the lunge rein in the arena, that kicking does no good to remove unwanted equipment, and that however much he kicks, the straps are still on him. Many horses make just one violent attempt to rid themselves of their crupper and then give up the unequal struggle. For this reason

51

it is so important to use correctly fitted, strong harness for breaking. Rotten leather and unsound stitching are almost sure to give way when put under stress and a great deal of harm may be done to a young horse if this happens.

Before going on to the next stage, the horse must be relaxed at all paces in both directions.

In this photograph the horse can be seen cantering on the correct leading leg. The off-hind is sweeping well under his body to propel him freely forward in a calm manner. He is not showing any signs of resistance to the crupper. His tail is being carried loosely. Animals who are planning on kicking usually clamp their tails down first.

The Breeching

It is best to put the breeching on with the roller, breast girth and crupper, and leave the horse in the stable to get used to the feeling of a strap around his quarters.

The loin strap of the breeching is threaded through the crupper back strap, which is attached to the roller. The breeching tugs, coming up from the seat of the breeching, must be so adjusted that the breeching is at the correct height around the hindquarters. It should lie below the widest part of the quarters and above the narrowest point, as seen in the next illustration. One which is fitted too high may get caught up under the horse's dock and cause kicking. One which is too low is likely to chafe and make the animal sore. It is important to fasten the breeching straps to the roller. It is unlikely that they will be long enough to reach, so a piece of cord or baler twine may have to be used on each side. This will hold the breeching seat in position and prevent it from being kicked upwards if the horse should take a violent dislike to its presence, which can happen if the horse is determined enough. The breeching should not be fastened too tightly as this can cause friction and make the horse uncomfortable.

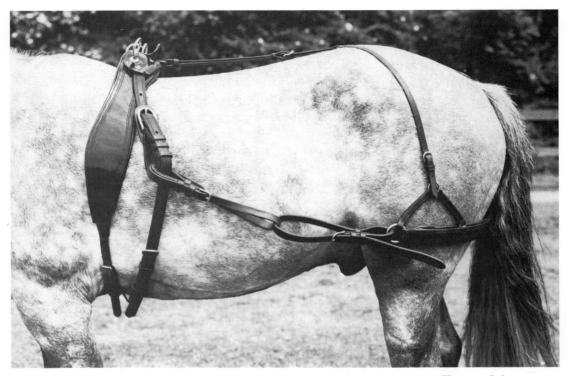

PHOTO 13　**The Saddle, Crupper and Breeching**

This illustration shows the driving saddle, crupper and breeching on the horse, in preparation for work on the circle.

The height of the breeching should be noted, as should the way in which the breeching straps are fastened to a second pair of straps so as to hold the breeching seat down.

The belly band is passed through a loop on the girth to prevent it from slipping back along the belly. If this happens it will act rather like a cinch, which is put onto a buck jumper at a rodeo in order to make him buck.

PHOTO 14 **Trotting in the Saddle, Crupper and Breeching**

The horse is seen here trotting happily round the arena. It will be noticed that he is looking out of the circle, which is incorrect. When these photographs were being taken, some young rabbits had a habit of emerging from the hedge with two cats in pursuit. These were, understandably, distracting the horse's attention from his trainer.

The activity of the off-hind leg can clearly be seen here, showing that he is working with adequate impulsion, even if it is being created by the disturbance.

55

PHOTO 15 **Cantering in the Saddle, Crupper and Breeching**

This illustration shows the horse going forward at the canter on the correct lead, at the stage when all four feet (but for the tip of one toe) are off the ground.

PHOTO 16 **Walking in the Saddle, Crupper and Breeching**

When the horse is prepared to work at all paces in the saddle, crupper and breeching in a calm and relaxed manner, as seen here, he is ready to be taken on to the next stage.

A Bridle with the Cavesson

It is sometimes found, when working small ponies up to the stage described so far, that their main interest lies in trying to eat any available grass when they are being worked. If this is causing a problem then it is best to place the bridle with the mouthing bit over the cavesson, as explained earlier. A piece of cord can then be tied to the bit ring on one side and run through the terrets of the saddle, before being fastened to the bit ring on the other side. This will not restrict the free forward movement provided that it is not tied too short, but it will prevent the animal from putting his head down and eating.

On no account should the trainer be tempted to try to force the animal's head into a position which he considers to be pleasing. It must be remembered that the horse's head cannot come into the correct place until he has built up the necessary muscles. The head position will improve when the horse has learnt to use his hocks and is going forward with plenty of impulsion. As a two- and three-year-old, the horse can only be shown the right direction for his head. Obviously, he must not be allowed to hollow his back and the top of his neck in a ewe-necked manner. Equally, he must not be forced to arch his neck, as this will inevitably lead to him bending his neck at his crest instead of from the poll and will result in overbending. This can cause tremendous problems. Horses which have their heads forced down and in, may drop the bit and overbend in order to relieve the pain which is being inflicted on their sensitive mouths. They will also shorten their stride. Therefore, incorrect work at this stage will probably ruin the horse for ever.

For a comparison between a four-year-old with a novice outline and a six-year-old with a more mature outlook, please turn to Photos 66 and 67 in which Loretto can be seen at both stages of training.

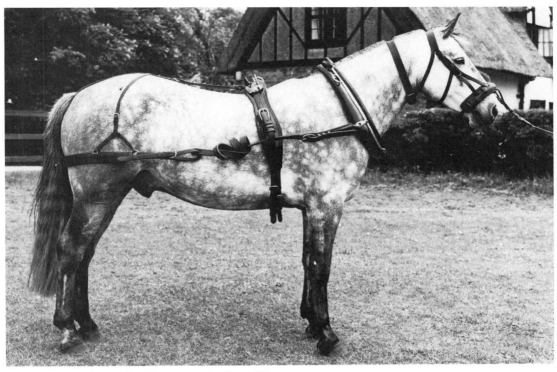

PHOTO 17 **The Collar and Saddle**

The collar and hames can be put on next. The collar should be put on upside down and the hames should not be attached at this stage. Care must be taken to stretch the collar widthways before it is passed over the young horse's eyes, so that it does not bruise him. It should then be left upside down on the horse's neck so that the hames can be laid on and buckled. It can then be turned and the hame-strap tightened. If the collar is forced over the horse's face with the hames in position, he may become frightened and difficult in the future. The traces are passed through the tugs and then wound round themselves. The breeching straps should be buckled through the crew holes of the traces. These are best fastened so that they are tight enough to give a certain amount of contact with the breeching on the quarters and the collar on the neck. They must not be buckled too tightly otherwise the horse will feel very restricted. He may also get chafed.

If a full collar is used, care must be taken to see that it fits correctly. A breast collar is easier to fit, so if a correctly fitting full collar is not available then it is preferable to use a breast collar.

A neck-strap is a helpful addition. It enables the horse to be held while the collar is being put on. If a full collar is pushed on or off over a headcollar, the lining may get damaged by the point of the headcollar buckle. This more often happens when the collar is being taken off than when it is being put on.

PHOTO 18 **Close-up View of a Full Collar**

Here can be seen a correctly fitting collar and hames. There is enough room at the side of the collar to get the flat of the hand between the horse's neck and the collar lining. If there is too much room the collar will rock from side to side. There is adequate space at the base to pass the whole hand between the horse's neck and the bottom of the collar. One which is too shallow will press against the wind-pipe and one which is too deep will ride upwards. The hames fit correctly into the groove between the forewale and aftwale. They are held in place by hame-straps at top and bottom.

The illustration also shows the neck-strap, which is preferable to a headcollar. Not only does it enable the horse to be held whilst he is harnessed and reduce the chance of headcollar buckle damage to the collar lining, but it can also remain on whilst the cavesson or bridle is fitted.

It is sometimes helpful to leave the neck-strap on the horse when he is being driven. There are two advantages: one is that the throatlash can be passed through the neck-strap as a safety precaution to keep the bridle in place when training. This really applies more to pairs, teams and tandems than to singles. Multiples of horses are inclined to rub their heads against either the pole-head or each other, and bridles can be pulled off. The wheeler of a tandem can be very susceptible to this if the leader comes round unexpectedly. It is never satisfactory to fasten the throatlash too tightly. A horse is unlikely to be persuaded to flex his jaw if the throatlash is cutting into his wind-pipe.

Another advantage of keeping the neck-strap on is that it provides an instant and convenient facility for holding the horse when the bridle is being taken off, during unharnessing.

It should perhaps be mentioned here that a blinkered horse should *never* have his bridle taken off whilst he is still in the vehicle. Sudden exposure to the cart behind him may cause him to step forward. The cart will follow and the horse will almost certainly take off. The writer has known this happen to the quietest of horses who had never been driven in an open bridle. The reason is that when the horse moves forward a small amount he sees, out of the corners of his eyes, the tops of two wheels which appear to be gaining on him. He then runs away. A very large number of accidents are caused each year by people who fail to obey this simple rule. Of course, horses who are used to working in open bridles are familiar with seeing the vehicle close behind them and do not mind.

There is sometimes a problem in keeping the bridle on a small pony owing to the amount of forelock, which causes the headpiece of the bridle to lie rather high. Such ponies often have very small ears, so the bridle is inadequately secured on the tiny head. It is a good idea to take a piece of the forelock and pass it over the poll, on top of the headpiece, before plaiting it into the piece of mane which lies behind the headpiece. This will help to prevent the bridle from being shaken or rubbed off. Some bridles are made with a second throatlash, similar to that seen on a cavesson, to prevent them from coming off.

PHOTO 19 **Close-up View of a Breast Collar**

A breast collar is much easier to fit than a full collar. It should lie below the bottom of the wind-pipe and above the point of the shoulder. It is preferable to have one with two dees and connecting leather to support the small tug which holds the neck-piece to the breast part. This type (shown in Photo 19) holds the collar straighter than do those with a single dee on the breast part.

The large dee at the bottom of the front of the collar enables a false martingale to be attached. This is not generally necessary when a horse is being broken. False martingales are used to keep the collar down and are employed with horses which show a lot of action. This extravagance can cause the collar to rise upwards on the shoulders. False martingales are, of course, always used with pair harness, but that is beyond the scope of this book.

The illustration also shows safes behind the trace tug buckles and hame tug buckles. These are an asset in preventing buckle wear on the traces and back-band. It is cheaper to replace worn safes than worn traces or back-band.

63

Note: the horse is wearing all the harness apart from the bridle and reins, with a full collar.

PHOTO 20 **Trotting on the Lunge in all the Harness with a Full Collar**

Horses do not seem to mind the addition of the collar, hames and traces. Here the horse can be seen going freely forward with his near-hind foot reaching well up into the track of the near-fore foot.

64

PHOTO 21 **Trotting on the Lunge in all the Harness with a Breast Collar**

The horse must go equally well in both directions before being taken on to the next stage.

If a breast collar is used, then a vehicle with a swingle tree is preferable. Solidly fixed trace hooks will cause the breast collar to move from side to side on the horse's shoulders and will quickly make a youngster sore. If he gets chafed he may refuse to go forward when he feels a weight on his shoulders and he will become 'collar shy'. He will then associate work in harness with pain and will cease to enjoy his lessons.

PHOTOS 22—23 **An Open Bridle with the Long Reins and Lunge Rein**

Photo 22 (taken from the offside) shows the pupil wearing a Fulmer cheekpiece jointed snaffle on an open bridle, in preparation for the early stages of long-reining. The lungeing rein is buckled to the offside of the bit for working on the left circle. It is put on as a precaution against letting go of the youngster if he should become frightened and try to get away.

Photo 23 shows how the lungeing rein is passed through the nearside ring of the bit, before going over the horse's head to buckle onto the offside ring. When it is put into use, the action of the bit resembles that of a gag snaffle. It is therefore extremely severe, and with this method it is possible to hold on to almost any horse. The advantage is that unless the horse tries to pull away, the rein remains slack and totally ineffective and harmless. Its presence gives great confidence to the trainer even though it may never be used.

PHOTO 24
Long-reining.

PHOTOS 24—27 **Long-Reining**

As soon as the horse is obedient to walk, trot, canter and halt on
the lunge rein, he can be introduced to work on the long reins,
during which time his mouth will be made. A mouth can easily be
ruined for life by misuse of the long reins. It is probably for this
reason that some people fix the long reins to rings at the side of
the cavesson instead of on to a bit. The disadvantage of this
method is that the horse can learn to lean on the trainer's hands
and can also get away more easily. Long-reining is a highly skilled
art and should not be executed by novices. The beginner has to
learn sometime, but it is preferable to practise on a mature animal
who has a *made* mouth. He, perhaps, will not get upset by clumsy
handling of the reins and lack of following through, whereas a
youngster will probably become frightened and muddled. This will

68

result in heavy-handed contact. The pupil will then be likely to overbend in order to avoid the discomfort. If the trainer positions himself incorrectly, the horse will probably stop and turn to face his handler. He will then pirouette, wrapping the reins round his chest, body and quarters, rendering the trainer helpless.

It is very important to have the horse obedient to the voice before he is long-reined so that it is not necessary to pull hard on his mouth in order to slow him down. It should be possible to bring him from canter to trot, to walk and halt, with the voice, combined with a bare minimum of pressure on the reins. Equally, he will learn to turn easily and change the rein, which will *make* his mouth because he will know what is expected of him. During the change of rein he will automatically go off on the circle from the centre of the arena providing that the trainer positions himself correctly.

PHOTO 25
*Following through
when long-reining.*

69

PHOTO 26

The horse is turned off the track to begin the change of rein.

For long-reining a youngster with an unmade mouth, it is best to use a jointed, cheekpiece bit such as a Fulmer snaffle. Such a bit cannot get pulled sideways through the mouth when there could be considerable sideways pressure on the horse's face during the first lesson in turning.

When the long reins are first buckled onto the bit they are passed through the saddle terrets, from the bit, to the trainer's hand. This position gives a direct contact with the mouth, from the terrets, and is similar to that which will be felt by the horse later when he is put to a cart or is being ridden. Another method of long-reining used by some trainers is to pass the long reins through low dees on a roller and to have the outer rein running round the horse's quarters. Some experts claim that the advantage of this method is that the quarters can be held onto the circle by the outer rein. The author's argument against this theory is that it

PHOTO 27
Going off on the right rein.

is not possible to obtain an even and light contact with both reins if the outer rein is lying against the horse's quarters. Also, this method can result in the horse carrying his head very low, which may lead to overbending. The method which is illustrated here has been used by the author on a large number of horses with success. It produces obedient and light-mouthed animals.

Great care should be taken to use very light reins. Heavy reins, or those with heavy buckles, can make a horse overbend by their sheer weight. Those seen in the photographs are tandem leader reins. They weigh 1lb 10oz (0.73kg) each and are 24 feet 6 inches (7.4m) long. They have proved to be too heavy for some very light-mouthed, small ponies and therefore cause overbending. They are, however, ideal for average animals over 13 hands high.

When the horse is first introduced to working on the long reins, as previously mentioned, it is a good idea to put a lungeing rein on

71

as well, as an insurance policy against letting go or getting into a muddle. If the horse gets wound up in the long reins then these can be dropped and the lunge rein used to hold the horse. He can be unwound and another attempt made to master the difficult art.

It is best to use the method of fixing the lungeing rein to the bridle as described earlier and illustrated in Photos 22 and 23. It is preferable to buckling the rein directly to the inner bit-ring, which can result in the whole bit and then the cheekpiece being pulled through the animal's mouth if he tries to get away from his trainer. Another method, which is also unsatisfactory, is to pass the rein through the inner ring, over the chin groove and buckle it to the outer ring. If the horse should pull, this will put greater pressure on the outer ring than on the inner ring, and the horse will turn out of the circle. The lunge will then lie along his ribs and quarters, rendering the trainer helpless. A coupling strap, buckled onto both rings, onto which the lunge is fastened, is another possibility, but this does not bring the horse towards the trainer as easily as in the author's preferred method. It is possible to leave the cavesson on and have the bridle and long reins on top, with the lunge attached to the cavesson, but it is inclined to get in the way of the cheeks of the jointed bit and cause pinching. The disadvantage of having a lunge rein on the bit as well as the long reins, is that changes of rein cannot be executed. When it is desired to send the horse round in a different direction, he has to be stopped first and the lunge rein has to be changed to the other side. So once the horse has become accustomed to the long reins, it is best to take the lunge off. If there is any doubt, to begin with, it is safest to leave one long rein out of the terret for the first few days. It can lie directly to the hand when the horse is going in one direction, resting under the terret on the pad when the horse is going the other way.

The important thing to remember when long-reining is that it is essential to follow the horse with the feet, as explained later, maintaining a steady contact with the hands. Working a horse on a true circle on long reins is highly skilled. The secret is in following through with the hands. The inner rein governs the bend and the outer rein governs the pace. So, if the horse is to be slowed

72

down, the outer rein should be used with stronger contact than the inner rein in order to keep the horse on the circle. The most usual fault which beginners make is that they get in front of the horse causing him to check in his pace. It is essential to keep towards the horse's inner hip. Another fault is the failure to maintain a very light but steady hand. Anyone who is clumsy with his hands will either stop the horse from going forward or will cause him to overbend. Usually, the weight of the reins, as they lie in a loop between the terrets and the trainer's hands, will give sufficient contact.

Careful work on the long reins is very valuable for teaching the horse correct paces and for developing his 'top line' (head, neck, back and quarters) to the desired shape. He can be driven forward with the whip and voice onto a light hand and his head carriage will gradually go into the right direction, as seen in Photo 25. This work is useful throughout the whole of the horse's life as a method of schooling to correct his way of going. It has the great advantage that the trainer is able to see where the horse is putting his feet and whether or not he is tracking up correctly. Also, his head position can be noted. Unlike a ridden horse, a harness horse does not have to adjust his balance to carry a weight on his back, so providing that he is put to a reasonably light cart and driven on surfaces which are not too holding, the way in which he goes when put to a vehicle should be similar to the way in which he has been working on the long reins. Therefore, the type of training which is carried out at home on the circle will relate to the way in which the horse goes when he is taken into the show ring or dressage arena. He will understand what is required when he is asked the question and should give the desired answer.

A very high degree of training can be carried out on long reins. It is possible to obtain such advanced movements as piaffe, passage and flying changes, though of course this work is not within the scope of a book on breaking to harness. It is mentioned in order to make the reader realize the potential value of long-reining.

There are various methods of holding the reins for long-reining. They can be held like riding reins, or sulky driving reins, with one in each hand. The disadvantage of this is that the outer rein is altered when the whip is uséd. They can be held like driving reins, in the left hand with the nearside rein over the index finger and the offside rein under the middle finger. The right hand is placed on the reins, in front of the left hand, with the middle and third fingers between the reins. The whip is held between the index finger and thumb of the right hand at an angle of 45° across the body to drive the horse from left to right. In going from right to left, the whip has to be held on the right in order to send the horse forward. (See Photo 25).

It is best to walk in a small circle as the horse works round on the outer track. The horse should be kept on as long a rein as possible. If the trainer tries to work the horse on a short rein he will find that he is not able to keep up if the horse accelerates and he will either let go or restrict the horse.

The trainer should try to follow the horse on an inner circle, maintaining a steady contact with his hands as the horse works round the outer track. He should be taken up and down through the paces and made to halt as required.

Changing the rein, i.e. going in the opposite direction, can cause problems to the newcomer to long-reining. This must first be executed at the walk (see Photo 26). Any attempt to carry out a change of rein at the trot will result in the horse being hauled round. This will muddle and frighten him and damage the sensitive bars of his (as yet unmade) mouth. When the change of rein is planned, the horse must be brought down to a calm walk. The trainer should shorten his reins and walk quite close to the horse, keeping almost behind, and just to the inside of, his quarters. For a left turn, the contact on the left rein must be increased and that on the right rein decreased. The right cheekpiece of the bit will press against the horse's face, which should turn him to the left. The trainer must keep the horse going forward towards the centre of the arena and must step across behind the horse, at the same time releasing the left rein and increasing the contact on the right rein. The horse, on seeing the trainer to his right, will automatically turn in that direction. It is here that previous correct work on the lunge will pay dividends. The horse must now be sent forward and he will go round on the right rein (see Photo 27). The secret of this movement lies entirely with the positioning of the trainer and his ability to keep the horse going forward. Lack of impulsion usually results in the horse stopping and turning to face his handler. It is at a time like this that he will wrap the reins around his chest, ribs and quarters as he continues, through the pressure of the inner rein, to turn in a tight circle. Once he has done this he resembles a parcel and is free to go. No amount of pulling will hold him.

In a change of rein the position of the whip must be altered as the horse changes direction. In Photos 26 and 27 it is being held downwards like a riding whip, coming out of the back of the hand, in order not to stop the horse from going forward by having it pointing in front of him. This is particularly important in Photo 27, when the change of rein is being completed and the horse is going off to the right. Photo 28 (dragging long traces) shows how the whip should be held across the body, like a carriage driving whip, in order to send the horse forward from left to right.

It is the early work at the walk, in repeated changes of rein, which makes the horse's mouth responsive. He learns to pay attention to his trainer's hands and soon reacts to the slightest touch to turn across the centre. There is no need to haul on his mouth to decrease pace because he will come back mainly on the vocal command. This can be lightly backed up with increased contact on the reins. The horse will soon learn to decrease his pace as a result of slight pressure on his mouth.

A Fulmer snaffle is ideal for this early training owing to its thick mouthpiece, which is relatively mild on the tongue and bars, combined with the cheeks for teaching him to turn. Some horses find the nutcracker action too severe. They draw their tongues back towards the throat and then try to get the tongue over the top of the bit to relieve the pressure. The horse must not be allowed to put his tongue over the bit. It is a habit which is easily acquired. Once discovered, it will become a nuisance. Putting the bit higher in the mouth sometimes prevents the horse from getting his tongue over, but this is not really very satisfactory with a young horse because it will make him uncomfortable. He may

then work with his mouth open and he might start to shake his head in an effort to avoid the pain. He may become sore at the corners of his mouth. It is far simpler to change the bit to one with a straight or half-moon bar. A rubber tongue plate (see Figs 2(a) and 2(b)) can be threaded onto the bit to prevent the horse from putting his tongue over it. As the bit can then be placed lower in the mouth, the horse will be more comfortable and he will probably soon stop trying to get his tongue over. The tongue plate can later be removed.

Once the youngster will obey the demands of his trainer to stop and turn, he can be taken out for walks with the long reins. It is advisable to replace the lunge rein in the way described earlier, as a safety precaution. It is a good idea to long-rein the horse along the lanes and tracks where he will first pull his cart. He will then get a chance to see things which could frighten him. It is better by far to let him have a good look at this stage, than to make him face too much when he is first put to a vehicle.

This work, at the walk, is advantageous in that it will develop the pace which is so often neglected. The horse must be made to trust his trainer, so that he gets used to answering commands from behind. When he is afraid and reluctant to pass a strange object, he should be driven, if possible, rather than led, so that he learns to obey his driver and does not rely on someone going to his head every time something frightens him.

Dragging Long Traces

PHOTO 28

Dragging long traces whilst wearing a full set of harness and an open bridle. Note the position of the whip sending the horse forward to the right.

As soon as the youngster can be long-reined both on the circle and out along the lanes, without drama, he can be introduced to the sight and sound of something behind him.

An old pair of traces can be tied with baler twine, by the tug buckle holes, to the crew holes of the traces which are already on the harness. These traces should be passed through the shaft tugs and the breeching. The old traces are then secured. It is essential to tie together the ends which are lying on the ground, to prevent them from flying apart when the horse works on the circle. The breeching straps must be fastened, as before, to a second pair of straps which are buckled onto the tugs.

If the horse has an exceptionally quiet temperament, he can

PHOTO 29
Dragging long traces.

start this work whilst he is still wearing a cavesson, as seen in Photo 29.

It is probably safest, however, with nearly all horses, to begin this work after he has been given considerable training on the long reins, so that he will be more easily controlled if he gets frightened.

Little can be done with a horse in a cavesson, if he rushes round the circle in an effort to run away from the traces, which he is convinced are chasing him. The only hope will be to pull him into the middle of the school in order to stop him. If he is afraid, he is unlikely to obey the commands of his trainer to walk and halt. The damage which may be done mentally could be considerable. So if there is the slightest doubt, it is best *not* to work the horse as is seen here. He must be worked with the long reins and the lunge rein buckled onto the bridle. He can then be more easily checked if he tries to take off. He will also have experienced many more hours of training once he has been worked on the long reins, and he is therefore less likely to be frightened. The young horse often gets to a stage when he is so confident that he is prepared to tolerate most of his trainer's requirements without making too much fuss. He will probably accept the sight and sound of the long traces following him. He will soon discover that the noises are harmless and will take no further notice.

Once he has settled to the work on the circle he can be taken out on the same routes along which he has recently been long-reined. There will be additional sounds of the traces dragging through gravel, puddles and leaves, etc.

PHOTO 30
The motor tyre.

PHOTOS 30–31 **The Motor Tyre and Too Much Weight on the Traces**

Once the horse is working confidently on the long reins, dragging the long traces, he is ready to pull a motor tyre.

If he is of a quiet nature, he can draw the tyre whilst wearing an open bridle. If, however, he is of a type which is nervous or flighty, it is safer to prevent him from looking behind by putting on a blinkered bridle, which is described later.

Quiet ponies are often happy to draw such a load in an open bridle. The advantage is that they gain great confidence by being able to look back and see the motor tyre behind them when it makes a variety of noises as it goes through, say, puddles or gravel, or hits a twig. The pony soon realizes that such noises are harmless and often becomes extremely quiet. However, hot-blooded animals will probably not stand the sight of such an object which is apparently chasing them. They can become so

PHOTO 31
*Too much weight on
the traces.*

frightened that they are unlikely ever to accept such work.

Horses of this type *must* be put into blinkers before being asked to pull a load of any kind. It is often a good idea to enlist the help of an assistant to hold onto and lean back against a pair of long traces, in order to introduce the youngster to the feeling of a weight on his collar, in preference to using a motor tyre. Photo 31 illustrates this procedure. It will be seen how too much weight on the traces has caused the horse, Ali, to throw up his head and hollow his back. It is important not to ask the young horse to pull too heavy a weight in the early stages. He will probably stop when he discovers that he is being held back by an excessive load against his unmuscled shoulders. When he is asked to go on he may find that the only way to move the load is to hurl himself against it with a kangaroo-like jump. This can quickly become a habit and he will then always start moving a load by

81

putting his head up and hollowing his back before leaping forward. Broken equipment may be the result. It is quite likely to lead to rearing and may even cause the horse to lie down. In any case, a horse who goes in this manner will never be pleasant to drive when conditions are testing, as he will find it almost impossible to pull a heavy load with his head up and his back hollowed. He will probably jib and will be unreliable.

The youngster should be encouraged to move a load by lowering his head and putting his shoulders into his collar as he walks calmly forward.

A motor tyre is ideal for this training with an averagely quiet horse.

Photo 33 shows the youngster learning to lean into his collar to pull the tyre, which he finds he is able to move quite easily. This work will give the horse confidence and as the load which he is asked to pull is increased gradually as his training progresses, he will eventually be willing to draw considerable weights. In later years, he will haul his load up hills or through deep going with confidence and without fuss.

The size of the tyre used should relate to the strength of the animal being trained. It will be found that a tyre from a Mini is large enough for a young Welsh Mountain type of pony, whilst a Land Rover tyre is suitable for a Welsh Cob type.

The advantage of a tyre over a light log is that it drags steadily along the ground. A light log is inclined to bounce and can, if the horse leaps forward, fly into the air and hit the horse on the hind legs. A heavy log can cause too much drag. It is best to put a chain round the tyre as rope wears out too quickly with the friction caused by it being pulled along the road. A ring should be fixed to the end of the traces. A rope with a spring clip can then be hooked onto the chain.

If the horse is nervous, it is best for the trainer to long-rein him whilst the assistant walks alongside or behind the trainer, dragging the tyre by the rope. This is an exhausting business for the assistant but is essential if the horse is frightened. He will feel 'protected' if the trainer walks between him and the tyre. He will eventually realize that the tyre is harmless.

82

PHOTO 32 **The Tyre Held by the Assistant**

When the horse is first asked to pull the tyre it is again a help to have an assistant.

The end of the rope is passed through the ring at the end of the traces. The assistant takes most of the weight of the tyre as the horse is asked to 'Walk on' round the arena.

The trainer can concentrate on holding the long reins and the lunge. If the horse should become jumpy, the assistant can let go of the rope and the tyre will be released instantly.

PHOTO 33 **The Horse Leaning into his Collar**

Gradually, the horse can be asked to take the full weight of the tyre, though the assistant is still holding the rope so that it can be released if necessary. The trainer is controlling the horse with the long reins and voice. The lunge rein is fixed on purely as a safety precaution. The horse can be long-reined out along the lanes like this.

PHOTO 34 **The Trainer has Fixed the Tyre to the Traces**

It is essential that the horse should learn to stand unheld by the head, whilst the tyre rope is tied to the traces. Control is maintained through the voice, long reins and lunge from behind the horse. This will teach him to stand unheld whilst he is being put to a cart when he is fully trained. If he should try to walk away he can easily be checked with the long reins and it may surprise the horse that his trainer has control even though he is some distance away from the horse's head. It is a great mistake to get into the habit of asking someone to hold the horse by the head whenever he is required to stand still.

PHOTO 35　**Pulling the Tyre**

Here the youngster can be seen pulling the tyre round the ring. He is quite calm and happy and is going forward in a relaxed manner. On no account should the horse be asked to trot whilst pulling the tyre on the circle. The tyre will almost certainly start to bounce about and this will probably frighten the horse, who may then try to run away from the tyre. Once he begins to canter the tyre will become airborne and will fly out sideways causing havoc.

PHOTO 36

PHOTOS 36—37 **The Horse in a Blinkered Bridle at the Walk and Trot**

If the horse is of a nervous disposition and unlikely to tolerate the sight of an object like a tyre close behind him, then he must be long-reined in a blinkered bridle before being asked to pull the tyre.

Some horses become very nervous when a closed bridle is first put on them. For the first time in their lives they cannot see to the side or behind and they become jumpy. Great care should be taken not to frighten the horse. Some people are extremely careless about the way in which they lead a blinkered horse out of the stable. If he is not brought out in a straight line he may catch the shaft tugs or his hip on a door post. He will then become nervous of going through doorways and probably try to rush. This usually results in the horse hitting himself harder, which makes

87

PHOTO 37
The horse in a
blinkered bridle at
the trot.

matters worse.

It is safest to put the bridle on outside the stable. The neck-strap is a great help for this. Care must be taken when leading the horse to the school to ensure that he does not walk into anything, such as a wheelbarrow, which he would normally see and avoid.

Before the horse is asked to pull the tyre in the blinkered bridle he must be taken through all the stages of work described earlier so that he is brought up gradually to accept the blinkers.

To summarize: he should first be long-reined in the blinkered bridle on the circle. Photo 37 shows the horse working happily at the trot in the blinkered bridle. He should then be taken out for walks along the lanes. Next he can be asked to drag the traces on the circle and then out along the lanes. Once he is fully confident he can be introduced to the sound of the tyre being dragged behind by an assistant, before it is finally attached to the traces for work on the circle.

He must *not* be asked to pull the tyre at the trot on the circle.

PHOTO 38
*Pulling the tyre on
the circle.*

PHOTOS 38—39   **Pulling the Tyre on the Circle**

Photo **38** shows the horse, in full harness with a blinkered bridle, pulling the motor tyre round the school. The lunge rein is fastened to the bridle, as well as the long reins. The horse is listening to the sound of the tyre and appears to be apprehensive. He is not going forward as freely as he should. His head is up and his back is stiff.

In Photo **39** the horse is seen to be going more calmly.

89

PHOTO 39
*A further stage of
pulling the tyre on
the circle.*

90

PHOTO 40
Halt on the track.

PHOTOS 40—41 **Halt on the Track and in the Centre of the Arena**

Photo 40 shows the horse in a happy frame of mind, standing unheld on the track of the circle.

The horse must learn to halt wherever required. In Photo 41 he is seen standing off the track, showing that he is willing to obey the commands of his trainer without question. When he looks like this he is ready to be taken out onto the lanes.

PHOTO 41
*Halt in the centre of
the arena.*

PHOTO 42 **On the Road with the Tyre**

When the horse is first taken out onto the road, with a motor tyre, it is a good idea to have an assistant who can hold the untied rope so that the tyre can quickly be released if there is need.

PHOTO 43 **Going for a Walk with the Tyre**

The horse can now be taken for walks pulling the tyre. It is advisable to keep the lunge rein attached to the bridle so that the horse can be held by this if an emergency arises. It is a great mistake to assume that because the horse is progressing quietly there is no danger of letting go of him if something happens to frighten him. At this stage it is almost impossible not to let go of the horse if the only control is with the long reins through the terrets. A loose horse, galloping across country, with a motor tyre attached to his traces, is not to be recommended. The result could set the horse back several months in his training. Horses never really forget or fully recover from a serious fright such as this.

94

When he is quiet enough, the horse should be asked to jog *for a few strides in a straight line*, along the road, with the tyre attached. This is essential in order to get him used to the rather uneven sounds and feel of a weight which he cannot see. It will be similar to that of a cart when it is pulled over rough ground, so it is safer to get him used to this with a tyre rather than to wait until he is put to a vehicle.

PHOTOS 44—45 **The Approach of Traffic and Passing a Lorry**

It is essential that the horse is trained to be unafraid of traffic before he is put to a vehicle. Modern road conditions do not allow for traffic-shy horses. The consequences of a harness horse whipping round can be serious or even fatal. It is a good idea to find a field which is adjacent to a busy main road, where the horse can be left for several months to contemplate the constant stream of heavy traffic. Not everyone has access to such a facility, in which case the horse will have to be ridden along roads where he will meet lorries and similar large vehicles. When introducing the youngster to traffic, it is best to go out with a quiet horse which is ridden by a friend. The youngster can then be taken alongside the

schoolmaster to take note of his lack of fear. Of course, if the trainer already has one horse which is traffic-proof, he can ride that one and lead the youngster alongside on the inner side. Later, they can be driven as a pair with the youngster tucked away from the traffic, on the nearside, in the early stages. Not everyone, though, is fortunate enough to have a second driving horse, a pair carriage and pair harness.

Small ponies, which cannot be ridden by an adult for traffic-proofing, create more of a problem. Long-reining in an open bridle is quite a good method. It is advisable to walk to the right of the pony, keeping him well to the left-hand side along the road. Approaching traffic is more likely to slow down on seeing someone walking in the middle of the lane. Drivers can then be thanked when they draw alongside. Most drivers understand the situation and are willing to co-operate. It is a help to wear one of

97

the orange-coloured over-vests with 'Caution — Young Horse' written on the front and back, which the British Driving Society has for sale. It must be remembered that the wearing of such a garment does not give the trainer the excuse not to acknowledge a driver's kindness in slowing down or stopping. Far too many horse owners neglect the common courtesy of thanking drivers. They only have themselves to blame, if, on the next occasion that they are out, the same driver does not bother to slow down. It is, however, more likely that the next horseman who is seen by the offended driver will be the one to suffer.

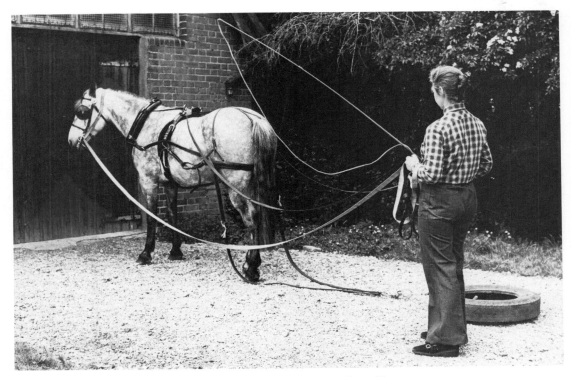

PHOTO 46 **Putting to the Tyre, Facing the Garage Door**

Once the horse is being taken for daily walks pulling the motor tyre, it is a good idea to accustom him to being put to the tyre facing a high obstacle such as a wall or, as here, a garage door, to prepare him for the initial stages of being put to a vehicle in a similar position. He will then learn to stand quietly in this place. He can be kept facing the door by the trainer holding the long reins and lunge with one hand whilst the tyre is tied with the other hand.

PHOTO 47 **Ali in the 'Walrond' Wheel-less Cart**

When the author broke Ali to harness, the problem regarding which vehicle to use for his first introduction to a cart caused considerable worry. He was an exceptionally difficult horse with a particularly nervous temperament. His potential brilliance was the sole reason for continuing with his education. It was thought that he might take off and get away in a wheeled-vehicle, so it was decided that if some kind of vehicle with skids instead of wheels could be devised, it might be safer for all concerned. Ali could then be swung round and the 'vehicle' would slide sideways. So a wheel-less cart was constructed by the author's husband, from elm suckers, nails and baler twine. Ali was put to this construction and long-reined for many miles during several weeks. The confidence gained by both horse and trainer was considerable and eventually

100

he was put to a wheeled-vehicle without any trouble. He subsequently became a big winner in private driving classes.

In many ways, the wheel-less cart was an intermediate step between the motor tyre and a wheeled-vehicle. It would, for example, move sideways when moving forward and not restrict the horse's quarters in a sideways direction, in the way in which a wheeled vehicle does. This was particularly important in a tight turn.

PHOTO 48

PHOTOS 48—50 **Putting to a Cart for the First Time**

When the horse is obedient and calm in all the preceding stages he can be put to a cart. He must be carefully prepared for this important occasion, as must those who are enlisted to help. On no account should the trainer attempt to put the horse to a vehicle on his own. If anything goes wrong at this stage the horse will probably be ruined for life. He should be worked on the circle beforehand and then be long-reined, pulling the tyre. People in the neighbourhood must be warned of the intentions so that they do not choose the very moment that the horse is being put to, to start up a chain-saw or let out the dogs.

The assistants must be thoroughly briefed on the putting-to procedure so that they are fully conversant with what they have to

102

PHOTO 49
The cart is drawn up.

do. If the weather conditions deteriorate, the plans must be delayed.

The vehicle must be a two-wheeler. Four-wheeled vehicles are not as safe with a young single horse owing to the fact that if the horse turns round, the front wheels will articulate and then, once the fore-carriage has come round as far as it can, depending on whether the vehicle has quarter, half or full lock, it is likely to turn over. Alternatively, the shafts may break. A two-wheeler is more likely to spin round with the horse, as the inside wheel rotates backwards and the outer wheel forwards. Of course, in the days when hundreds of horses were being broken to harness, a four-wheeled breaking-cart, such as a skeleton break, was used and the youngster put in alongside an older schoolmaster on the other side of the pole. Now, most people have neither a school-master nor a skeleton break. These vehicles were solidly built,

103

PHOTO 50
The shafts are put into
the tugs.

with just a driver's seat which was placed high above the horses' quarters. The substantial wheels were set wide apart on a perch undercarriage and there was a platform on which the groom stood behind the driver. The pole was padded with leather, as was the splinter bar. The old fashioned two-wheeled breaking carts had long shafts and were sturdy constructions. Unfortunately, now, most people have to make do with whatever vehicle is to hand. It is for this reason that such care must be taken in the preparation of training the horse to pull a cart. After all, no one wants to see their valuable vehicle kicked to pieces.

If the horse has responded to the training as described, there is no reason why he should cause problems when he is put to, providing that no chances are taken at this vital stage.

The horse should be brought up to face a garage door, wall or similar obstruction and be held, on either side, by the trainer and an assistant. Two lunge reins should be put onto the bridle by the over-the-head method, as previously used, so that each person has one. The assistant on the offside controls the horse, whilst the cart is brought up to the horse by the trainer. A third person, at the back of the cart, is useful as he can steer the cart and take some of its weight. The trainer holds the nearside shaft and guides it into the nearside shaft tug. Great care must be taken to ensure that the tip is not dug into the horse's quarters. Such carelessness can cause unnecessary havoc. The assistant should take the offside shaft tip and put it into the offside tug.

Both the trainer and the assistant must be careful that they do not inadvertently pull the horse round with their lunge rein when they are reaching to put the shaft tip into the shaft tug. This is a common fault committed by novices when putting to.

PHOTO 51
The nearside trace is fastened.

PHOTOS 51—52 ## The Nearside and Offside Traces are Fastened

The nearside trace is first hooked onto the swingle tree by the trainer. The offside trace is then hooked onto the swingle tree.

It is essential to hook on both traces before the breeching is fastened. Then if the horse should move he will be secured to the vehicle, which will remain with him until the trainer and assistant quickly stop him. If, on the other hand, the breeching and trace is fastened on one side before the trace is hooked on the other side and the horse should move, he may begin to get halfway out of the cart before anyone can stop him. This particularly applies if a breast collar is used as it will slip sideways, which could make the horse frightened and cause difficulties.

106

PHOTO 52
*The offside trace is
hooked.*

PHOTO 53 **The Nearside Breeching Strap is Buckled**

Whilst the trainer is on the offside he can buckle the offside breeching strap round the shaft and trace before coming round to the nearside to buckle that breeching strap. It is best to use full breeching during the early stages of training because the seat of the breeching is in some kind of contact with the horse's quarters all the time. It should be fitted so that it lies below the widest part of the hind quarters and above the narrowest part. If it is fitted too high there is the danger of it riding up under the dock, which can cause disastrous results. The horse will probably try to clamp his tail down onto it and may start to kick. Once he has contacted the splinter bar with a hind foot he will frighten himself and probably kick all the harder; he may even continue to kick until he has removed himself from the vehicle. If the breeching is too low it may cause the hind legs to be pushed forward and result in the horse slipping. False breeching is not a good idea until the animal is thoroughly conversant with his job. This is because false breeching lies back away from the horse when he is in draught but when he slows down or stops it will suddenly touch his quarters and probably frighten him. At a later stage it is ideal for everyday work, when it can be left on the vehicle apart from when it is taken off for cleaning, thus cutting down the putting-to time considerably.

PHOTO 54   **The Belly Band is Tightened**

The belly band is best left a little loose when the shafts are being put through the tugs, leaving the tugs more manoeuvrability for putting to. The belly band is buckled tighter in the early stages of breaking than it is later when the horse is fully broken. As a precaution it is safer to buckle it slightly tighter for the first few days of taking the youngster out. If the horse rears and swings to one side, it is quite easy for him to come down with the shafts across his back if the belly band is buckled too loosely. Of course, it must not be buckled so tightly that the shafts are held rigidly, as this would prevent the vehicle from balancing correctly. Ideally, the shafts should float in the tugs but at this stage it is quite a good idea to put a little weight onto the youngster's back.

110

A kicking strap can be fastened over the horse's loins as an additional precaution. It is fixed to the shafts, about half way between the false and full breeching dees. The strap, or rope, is then passed over the horse's back and fastened onto the opposite shaft. Its presence may help to hold the horse's quarters down if he should try to kick. It must not be fixed too tightly, or it may actually cause the horse to kick if he feels restricted. A rope halter can be improvised as a kicking strap. The headpiece is threaded through itself onto one of the shafts. The rope is passed over the horse's loins through a loop on the crupper, before being tied to the opposite shaft in a quick-release knot. If regular use is being made of a kicking strap, then dees should be put onto the shafts to hold it in place and a proper strap and buckles should be employed.

It is perhaps worth mentioning here that the youngster is best left unshod for the first few days of being put to a cart. His attention will be diverted to his feet if he is taken on tracks rather than made-up roads or grass. This can be of considerable help to the trainer. The horse must not, of course, be taken for great distances, which would make his feet really sore. He should be shod as soon as he appears to be moderately safe in the vehicle. If he is asked to work when his feet have become very sore, he may well resent this type of employment and refuse to go forward. This would result in nappiness which would otherwise not have occurred.

PHOTO 55 **Turning the Cart and Moving Off**

The disadvantage of putting to facing an obstruction is that the
youngster has to be turned sideways when he is asked to move off
for the first time. The advantage, however, outweighs the disadvantage of having to turn. It is essential that the turn should be
made as easy as possible for the horse so that he does not get
frightened. When the command 'Walk on' is given, the trainer must
bring the horse round with the left hand on the lunge rein whilst
the right hand pulls the shaft towards him by its tip. The assistant
must push the offside shaft tip with the left hand whilst holding
the lunge rein with the right hand. The trainer is responsible for
the control of the horse; the assistant is only there for emergency
and should not give signals or commands to the horse unless the

112

need arises. Therefore, the assistant should hold his lunge rein so that there is almost contact with the horse's mouth, but not quite. The second assistant should steer the cart from behind as much as he can so the horse is not impeded too much in his turn. This will be the first time in the horse's life that he has tried to turn and discovered that his quarters are held against the offside shaft. Providing that care is taken as described here, there will be no problem. The horse will quickly learn to stand still when he is being put to and he will soon learn how to turn the vehicle without help. Within about three days it will be possible to put to facing away from the garage door and he will stand still whilst traces, breeching and belly band are buckled. He will then walk quietly forward, being led, whilst turning any bends in the drive or track leading to the road. If, however, he is not carefully introduced to the art of turning the cart he may, in later life, become very frightened and resist tight turns when under stress.

PHOTO 56 **A Nervous Youngster Turning the Cart**

Here Ali can be seen showing the stiffness down the spine and legs which is so typical of a nervous youngster in turning a vehicle.

114

Reining-Back

On no account should the pupil be backed away from the obstruction he faced when putting to.

The horse should not be taught to rein-back until he is rising four years old. He should not, in any case, be driven for any great distances until he is at least four, so there should not be any need for him to know how to rein-back to command. If this movement is taught too soon, the horse may use it as an effective method of resistance to anything which he does not wish to do. A horse which runs back, with a cart behind him, can do a tremendous amount of damage to such things as parked cars.

Running back can also lead to rearing, which is almost impossible to cure entirely.

It should perhaps be mentioned here that anyone who is planning on driving on public roads is well advised to ensure that their third party insurance cover is adequate.

PHOTO 57   **Ready to Go Out on the Road**

Generally speaking, it is safer to take the youngster out on a quiet road or along a farm track, than to work him in a field. A wide open expanse of grass can cause excitement, whereas a horse will be more likely to remain calm if he can be led down a stony track. Knee pads are a sensible precaution. They take a few moments to put on and could save a blemish which may last for a life-time.

116

PHOTO 58 **Going Down the Drive**

On the way to the road the horse meets a turn in the drive and is helped by the trainer and assistant who bring the shafts round. A helper should be sent ahead to see that the road is clear at the gate.

A length of cord and a knife are carried on the cart for use in case of emergency.

117

PHOTO 59 **The Horse is Led Along a Quiet Road**

The trainer and assistant lead the horse along the lane, having helped him to turn the cart at the corner out of the drive.

Care should be taken whilst walking along the road that the shaft tip does not go into either person's back, if the horse should jump forward.

The youngster must not be asked to pull his cart very far during these early stages of training. His shoulders will become sore quickly. This is almost certain to result in reluctance to go forward, which may lead to nappiness. Also, his limbs will probably become permanently damaged if he is subjected to hard work before he has had time to grow and develop.

It is essential to choose a flat route which is either circular or

118

has a circular turning point, like a village green with a perimeter road. If the horse is taken along a road for just a few hundred yards (metres) and then turned round in the road and brought back, he will soon anticipate the turn for home. This will lead to all kinds of troubles and resistances. The author is fortunate to have a stony track through a wood, with a turning area at the end where there is an oval lawn and a surrounding drive. The total distance is about 500 yards (metres) and is ideal for walking two-year-olds when they are first put to a vehicle. It has been proved, repeatedly, to be quite far enough to establish confidence in both the horse and the trainer.

The two-year-old needs only to be taken along such a route on about four occasions, on consecutive days, providing that he is calm and unafraid, before being turned away for a year to grow.

On no account should he be taken out for long drives at this stage. It is often very tempting to do too much with a two-year-old who appears to be going quietly. The temptation, however, must be resisted. The animal will last for far longer if he is left to mature before he is worked hard.

As much care must be applied to taking the horse from the vehicle as was employed when he was put to. Everyone involved must know exactly the method which is to be used.

The youngster should be brought up to face a garage door, wall or similar construction, with the trainer leading him from the nearside and the assistant from the offside. The assistant should hold the horse whilst the trainer, who is also still holding a lunge rein, loosens the belly band. The nearside breeching strap is unbuckled. Then the offside breeching strap is unfastened. The offside trace can now be unhooked and either wound around itself or placed over the horse's back. The nearside trace is now unhooked and coiled up or put over the horse's back. The cart can then be pushed back, away from the horse, by the trainer. It is then taken by the second assistant.

If a kicking strap has been used then this must be undone before the belly band, breeching and traces are unfastened.

As the horse's education progresses there will be no need to face him to an obstruction.

PHOTO 60 **The Trainer Takes Up the Reins**

When the horse is going quietly, the nearside lunge rein can be taken by the assistant and the offside lunge rein can be removed. The trainer should pick up the driving reins and control the horse from alongside his quarters. It is a help to wear hogskin gloves. The reins are taken up in the driving position to give greater control. The nearside rein lies over the index finger of the left hand and the offside rein lies between the middle and ring fingers. The right hand is placed in front of the left, with the nearside rein over the middle finger and the offside rein under the third finger to assist the left in steering or checking the horse.

120

PHOTO 61 **Mounting for the First Time**

When mounting for the first time, it is important to do it whilst the vehicle is moving. The horse then hardly notices the extra weight and collar shyness is avoided. The reins should be held in the left hand with the loose end thrown over the forearm so that it does not get caught in the step in mounting.

It is usual to mount from the offside for private driving in Great Britain. On this occasion, however, it is safer to mount from the nearside. The trainer will already be on this side and the reins can remain in the left hand so do not have to be changed as they would if the driver were to mount from the offside.

The seat cushions *must* be strapped to the seat of the cart. Loose cushions are very dangerous because they can easily slide off the seat and throw the driver onto the road.

121

PHOTO 62 **The Driving Position is Taken Up**

The trainer is in control of the situation from the box, with the reins held in the left hand, which is supported by the right. The traditional method of handling the reins, as described earlier, is essential for full control. The left hand, with the reins on either side of the index and middle fingers, is the anchor hand. The ends of the reins lie down across the palm and are kept in position with the fingers lying over the top of them. The right hand is placed on the reins in front of the left. The whip is held at an angle of 45° to the reins (or at ten to twelve on the clockface), lying over the thumb muscle across the palm of the right hand. As this is the only means for creating forward impulsion, other than the voice, the whip must be held at all times. It is no use keeping it in the

122

whip socket until it is needed, in the hope that it can be got out and used when wanted. There just is not time to pick up the whip when a horse suddenly stops or tries to evade the wishes of his driver. Of course, if the whip should have to be used at this early stage it must be employed with discretion and well forward on the horse, so that it does not result in him kicking.

The right hand, in the position described, is used for turns to the right and left, for assisting the left hand in slowing down and shortening the reins as well as for applying the whip or giving signals. For a turn to the right, the whole of the right hand, still holding the whip, is placed over the offside rein, taking care to remove the index finger from over the nearside rein. A turn to the left is made by placing the right hand under the nearside rein. The left hand can be turned with the knuckles facing uppermost for a left turn and palm uppermost for a right turn. If a turn has to be made with the left hand only, because a whip signal is being given with the right hand, then the left hand can be turned upwards or downwards, as just described, for a slight turn, and brought towards the left hip for a sharper right turn and towards the right hip for a stronger left-handed turn. This has the effect of shortening the rein which is pulled towards the hip and lengthening the other. The horse should then turn readily. The reins can be shortened by either placing the right hand behind the left and sliding the left up the reins for the required amount, or by sliding the right hand up the reins and inching the left hand towards the right. This is only suitable for shortening the reins by small amounts as they will go into loops if any attempt is made to shorten them a great distance. A pulling horse is steadied with both hands working in unison with the right hand in front of the left.

The position of the driver's legs and feet is important. They should be kept at a fairly straight angle enabling strong purchase to be obtained with the feet against either the foot-board or foot-rest if the horse should start to pull. It is very difficult to hold a pulling horse if the legs are bent at right angles, at the knees, and almost impossible if the feet are not firmly pressed against a solid barrier like a foot-rest.

PHOTO 63 **The Assistant is Mounted**

When the horse is accepting his work, the assistant can mount. This should be done whilst the horse is walking so that he does not notice the additional weight. Obviously, it is only for the first few days that the assistant should have to climb into a moving vehicle.

It is sometimes a wise precaution for the assistant to keep the nearside lunge rein attached when he first mounts. Care must, however, be taken to see that it does not get caught under the shaft tip or on the rein rail and pull the horse round accidently. The lunge rein can be useful if an emergency should arise.

On one occasion, the author was driving a small young pony which started to kick. It got a hind leg over a shaft and the vehicle half turned over tipping the driver onto the road. Fortunately, the

124

lunge rein was attached and it was possible to hold the pony as it circled round. The cart righted itself as the pony got her leg back and the author remounted, unhurt, to continue the drive. The pony had learnt her lesson and did not repeat the performance.

Once the horse is happy in his work, he can be asked to move off from an unheld halt with both his driver and passenger sitting in the vehicle. If his early training has been carried out correctly this should be achieved quite soon.

The assistant must be prepared to dismount quickly and quietly whilst the vehicle is moving, in order to help to hold the vehicle back down a hill so that the young horse does not have to take all the weight. Help may be needed, too, up any incline which might otherwise cause a problem. The horse must never be made to feel that he cannot cope with the job which is being asked of him.

It is probably safest not to use a knee rug or apron at this stage. There is the danger of tripping over such an addition if there is need to dismount in a hurry.

A nylon whip is still used instead of a traditional holly whip. Holly whips are getting harder to find and are expensive to replace. They are very fragile and the tops can easily get broken. A youngster dragging a cart through some bushes can result in the top of the whip getting caught in a branch, which is almost certain to break either the stick or the quill.

PHOTO 64 **Standing in the Field**

Once the horse has worked quietly on the road he can be driven in the field. It is essential to drive the horse on grass before he is taken to a show. He will learn that the vehicle does not run as easily on turf as it did on the road and he will have to lean into his collar harder in order to start it. He will also have to get used to the vehicle hitting bumps and ruts in the ground which may, at first, frighten him as the vibration is transmitted to his back, from the saddle and shafts, and to his shoulders through the collar. Equally, the breeching may hit him more violently.

Whilst he is put to, he must stand unheld by the head (the driver will have hold of the reins if necessary) on grass without moving off or trying to eat.

126

He must continue to stand unheld whilst his driver mounts. On no account should passengers mount until the driver is seated and positioned on the box in such a way that he is in full control of the horse. Equally, on returning from a drive, the passengers should dismount before the driver so that he maintains full control until they are safely on the ground. It is extremely dangerous for passengers to be seated in the vehicle if the driver is not on the box to control the horse. A number of serious accidents have occurred because of failure to observe this golden rule.

PHOTO 65 **Trotting in the Field**

As soon as the horse has learnt to work at the walk in a calm and obedient manner on grass he can be trotted quietly.

It is best not to be tempted to ask the horse to extend on grass too soon, otherwise he will soon associate working on turf with extending and may start to get excited and pull.

When he can be worked confidently on grass he should be introduced to the sounds and sight of another horse pulling a cart behind, alongside and in front of him. Some horses get quite nervous when they first hear another turnout alongside, so this should be practised in surroundings with which the horse is familiar before he experiences the trauma of a crowded show-ground.

It will be seen in this illustration that the shafts of this vehicle (a speed cart, jogger, spinner or road cart) fit correctly for length. When the horse is in draught the back-band should hang at the perpendicular whilst the tugs are against the tug stops. The shaft tips should be level with the hames. When the horse is in draught the breeching should lie away from the hindquarters. When the horse is holding the cart down a hill it should be found that the breeching tightens round the quarters. The traces will hang slack and the back-band will go forward to about 40°. If, however, the breeching straps are too loose the tugs will force the back-band and saddle forwards towards the withers and the horse will take the weight on his tail via the crupper. This understandably could lead to kicking. There must be enough room between the quarters and the splinter bar to ensure that the horse does not get touched when pulling up or going downhill. There is a little too much upward slope on the shafts of the vehicle seen here. The seat should lie at the horizontal and in fact there is a slight slope. This could be cured by putting small blocks of wood between the axle and the springs, which would raise the body by an inch or so to make it level. This vehicle has been used for animals ranging from 11 hands to 15 hands and fits them all, with varying degrees of accuracy, for breaking purposes. It is light, quiet and runs easily.

Ideally, for breaking, it is preferable to have a vehicle with much longer shafts so that if a youngster starts to kick he will not contact the front of the cart.

PHOTO 66 **Four-Year-Old Cottenham Loretto at His First Show**

Here can be seen the four-year-old pony with a novice outline. His hind leg is well under him to propel him forward but his head is not being forced into position. He is being driven onward and shown the way to go with a steady hand, but he is not being held tightly into a restricted false outline, which would result in loss of forward movement and would shorten his stride.

This photograph was taken at the English Connemara Society's Show, where Cottenham Loretto made his debut and won his class.

PHOTO 67 **Cottenham Loretto as a Six-Year-Old**

This illustration shows Loretto, two years later, winning his class at the East of England Show. The increased impulsion and greater use of his hocks has resulted in a pleasing head carriage which has developed naturally. At no time was the head pulled into position by the driver's hands. It was pushed into position from behind with impulsion.

A pony who is confident in his driver is more likely to go in this manner than one who is apprehensive.

It will be noticed that he had no contact with the ground at the moment when the photograph was taken, demonstrating the lightness which was being achieved.

The vehicle shown is a Skeleton Gig.

131

PHOTO 68   **A Vehicle Which is Too Small for the Horse**

This specially taken photograph shows a horse which is much too large for its vehicle (a Norfolk Cart).

Such an equipage would be uncomfortable to drive because the driver and passenger would be tipped into a backward position. The danger of the horse being hit on the quarters by the dashboard is considerable. It is quite possible to break the dashboard on a horse which is put to a vehicle in this way, if a steep hill is descended. Another danger is the likelihood of the shaft tip getting caught under the horse's collar in turning.

132

PHOTO 69 **A Vehicle Which is Too Large for the Horse**

Here is seen an Essex Cart which is much too large for the pony. This shot was taken specially to illustrate the point.

One of the disadvantages of such an ill-fitting vehicle is that the weight of the carriage is being taken on the horse's back through the shafts via the saddle, back-band and tugs. If the horse were to be driven for any length of time in such a vehicle, with the light saddle which is shown here, he could get a sore back. Another disadvantage of such a combination is the downhill ride which would be given to the driver and passenger, resulting in considerable 'knee rock' at every trotting stride. The likelihood of catching the reins under the excessively long shaft ends would be considerable.

133

PHOTO 70 **A Vehicle Which is Incorrectly Balanced**

This illustration shows a Governess Cart which is unbalanced owing to the fact that the Whip is sitting too far back. It is important to adjust the weight in a two-wheeled vehicle so that the shafts float in the tugs. When the horse is trotting, the points of the tug buckles should ride up and down against the buckles. This ensures that there is no weight on the horse's back. If the vehicle is unbalanced, as is seen in this illustration (which was photographed specially to show the point), there is considerable upward pressure from the belly band against the horse's belly. If the belly band were to break, the vehicle would tip over backwards.

134

PHOTO 71 **Ali, a part-Arab stallion, at the Height of his Show Career**

PHOTO 72 **Alibi and Razali in Tandem**

Alibi and Razali driven by the author to a Ralli Car. In 1975 they became the first tandem to complete a three-day combined driving event. They are seen here crossing the river at the Lowther Driving Trials.